A MIND OF
MY OWN

A MIND OF MY OWN

KATHY BURKE

GALLERY BOOKS UK

London · New York · Amsterdam/Antwerp · Sydney/Melbourne · Toronto · New Delhi

First published in Great Britain by Gallery Books,
an imprint of Simon & Schuster UK Ltd, 2025

3 5 7 9 10 8 6 4

Simon & Schuster UK Ltd
1st Floor
222 Gray's Inn Road
London WC1X 8HB

www.simonandschuster.co.uk
www.simonandschuster.com.au
www.simonandschuster.co.in

Simon & Schuster Australia, Sydney
Simon & Schuster India, New Delhi

The authorised representative in the EEA is Simon & Schuster Netherlands BV,
Herculesplein 96, 3584 AA Utrecht, Netherlands. info@simonandschuster.nl

A CIP catalogue record for this book is available from the British Library

Hardback ISBN: 978-1-3985-4814-5
Trade Paperback 978-1-3985-5337-8
eBook ISBN: 978-1-3985-4815-2

Typeset by Palimpsest Book Production Ltd, Falkirk, Stirlingshire
Plate sections designed by Will Mower

Printed and Bound in the UK using 100% Renewable Electricity at CPI Group (UK) Ltd

For Nellie, Joan and all the sharers.

BEFORE I BEGIN

In the last ten years of his life my dad was sober, worked hard and loved to travel around Europe on coach trips. People who knew him during that time probably wouldn't recognise the man I talk about in the early chapters of this book. I think they're lucky. I would have loved to have known him as this latter man always but sadly this wasn't the case.

He was diagnosed with cancer in September 1993 and passed away in April '94. The day before he died, knowing things were now terminal and there wasn't much time for him left, we had a chat in the hospital, St Bart's, about this and that, searching for things to say. I piped up, 'I suppose I should try and stop smoking.'

'Oh yes,' he said, latching on. 'Promise me you'll give up the cigarettes.'

'I'll do my best,' I said. 'But not just yet.'

He smiled. 'Not just yet, no. You'll be too upset.' Then after a beat he said, 'You should try and write more. I loved that play you wrote. I like your acting but your writing is good. I wish I had been a writer.'

'It's hard, though, Dad,' I said. 'And it's a struggle knowing what to write about.'

'You could write about me,' he suggested.

I laughed wryly and said, 'You sure about that, mate?'

He let that sink in for a moment then shrugged and said, 'Sure, I won't be here. You knock yourself out.' It's taken me over thirty years but here we finally are. It's not all about him, of course, but Dad is the only ghostwriter involved with this book.

PART ONE

IDENTITY

When I was around eight or nine years old, my dad, Pat, arrived home early one evening with a busted nose and bruised ego. He'd been beaten up.

This wasn't unusual if he was on a drinking binge. A raging beast would often crash home, to disturb an already fitful sleep, the agonies of life streaming from his chaotic head down into his fists and feet.

But not in times of sobriety.

A couple of men had stopped him in the street, asking for a light for their cigarettes. They'd got him talking and, realising he was Irish, proceeded to give him a right good kicking.

When he told me what had happened I remember quite clearly an internal shock and then overriding fear.

I'd gleaned from news reports that the Irish were, as sung in a popular song by The Dubliners, 'Building Up And Tearing England Down' but surely not all of them?

Or should that be all of *us*?

Was I Irish? My community certainly felt so. Most of the kids I knew had at least one Irish parent and the teachers, priests and other adults on the edges of our childhood world were also mostly Irish. We went to Catholic schools and got bored during Catholic Mass. Catholic equalled Irish, as far as I was concerned.

But I was also a Londoner, born in Islington during the Swinging Sixties, so surely that would prevent me from getting beaten up in the street too?

There was the shift.

I didn't want to be Irish.

I wanted to be a 'cockney'.

I wanted to be tough and boyish and, more importantly, English.

The Irish were the butt of jokes on the telly. They were seen as 'thick', incapable of doing anything other than getting pissed up and tunelessly lamenting their sorely missed emerald homeland. And, in some ways, this was my dad. Not thick, but definitely drunk and a terrible singer.

He worked, but not consistently. As a binger he would often have days, sometimes weeks 'on the sick', which involved a note from our doctor informing whatever foreman on whatever building site Dad was working on at the time that he was too poorly for the graft – but it ensured he would still get his wage.

'Poorly' meaning 'hungover'. The worst kind. Delirium tremens.

A consistent pattern throughout my childhood was Dad being drunk, hungover and then, for a semi-peaceful time, dry.

Drunk. Hungover. Dry.

Repeat, repeat, repeat.

We were living with a lunatic.

Life hadn't been kind to him. I don't know much about Dad's own parents, beyond the fact his mother had tried to kill herself and was subsequently put in an asylum where she later died, and his father was himself a feared, raging beast who would drag Pat and his little brother, Joe, out of their schoolroom in Galway to work on his farm. There lies the trauma.

The two brothers left Ireland in the early 1950s, answering a call out for immigrants to England where there was plenty of work to be had. Dad went to London, Joe to Manchester.

Uncle Joe was gorgeous. Rosy-cheeked and chuckly. He and his family would sometimes visit us during the Easter holidays, and I can honestly say it's the only time I remember seeing my dad truly happy.

I watched Dad bathing his wounds at the kitchen sink. His shirt was off. Freckled back, tan lines and a whiff of Deep Heat ointment. I must've expressed my fears. Did people really get beaten up just for being Irish? He looked at me with a frown that I've inherited and said in his whiny brogue something that, as a boomer in 2025, I can now interpret as a lesson on the purposely misunderstood white privilege:

'At least we're not Black. Those feckers only knew I was Irish cos I opened my mouth. Derek from work can get a hiding on sight so think yourself lucky!'

See, certainly not thick.

I was often told how lucky I was. Lucky to have food on the table (although not always); lucky to be at a good school (primary yes, secondary not so much); and lucky to have a roof over my head (true as we were in affordable council accommodation).

I didn't feel lucky, though. I just felt worn out. I was constantly tired, with permanent dark shadows under my eyes. Maybe sharing a bedroom with Dad up to the age of ten had something to do with that?

I wasn't always living at home, though.

Our mum, Bridget, had died.

A kind and strong-minded woman from Cork, she'd met the younger-than-herself Pat at the Gresham Ballroom on Holloway Road.

They married in Camden and settled in Islington. Firstly, in a shared house with other Irish immigrants who would become friends, godparents, etc. and then into 'luxury': Halton Mansions, housing a two-bedroom flat with its own kitchen, bathroom and spacious living room situated on the ground floor of a four-tiered, three-rowed, red-brick, crumbling old mansion block.

We resided at one end of the middle row. Washing lines and bin chutes to the back of us, trees and patches of green splendour to the front.

Before the move, though, Pat and Bridget had two boys.

John, born in 1956, and Barry in 1958.

John recalls happy-ish times in the shared house. Apparently, Dad was always a scary grump but Mum was fun and doting, and the other families, the Costellos and the Mackies, were gorgeous. In another house across the road lived the Corcorans, who would later become a very important part of my life. Uncle Denny and Auntie Nellie would be my godparents.

As a kid I would've assumed that the men were pals with the men and the women were pals with the women, but I found out as a young adult that my mum and Denny were actually best friends back in Cork and had headed to London together.

I always felt close to Denny and discovering his closeness to my mother explained why.

He was such a sweet and quietly spoken man despite a mighty frame. His thick Cork accent was mostly incomprehensible to me. I imagined tiny birds fluttering around inside his top palate, forcing his words into gentle whistles and rolls.

Auntie Nellie, real name Esther, was and still is a forward-thinking, unjudgemental darling with wavy, tawny hair on top of her tiny frame. She's in her nineties now, her hair is a wondrous white. She loved a pressure cooker and I loved whatever was cooking inside it.

Pat, Bridget, John and Barry moved to Halton Mansions in 1962, I was born at the long-since-closed Royal Free Hospital on Liverpool Road in June 1964 and Bridget died from stomach cancer in December 1966 at the age of thirty-eight.

FAME I

Having a dead mum made me feel dead famous. Everyone seemed to know me and my business.

Teachers, social workers and the local Irish community put their heads together to come up with some sort of plan as to what should be done with me.

There was talk of adoption, something Dad wasn't too keen on, but then it was decided that I should remain with Uncle Joe, his wife Anne and their children in Manchester as I'd been taken there when our mum was in hospital.

Apparently, I screamed the place down. I was two years old and having none of it.

What was it that I didn't like? What was it that I missed?

There's a photo of myself, John and Barry that was taken professionally in a studio. The brothers are scrubbed clean and in their school uniforms. They're sitting on a posh-looking couch, me standing in the middle, with the boys holding my wobbly self up. White frilly dress, satin booties and a bald egghead. I was aged around one so our mum was still alive and no doubt organised it.

And was probably there.

Did she know she was sick by then?

I loved looking at the photo when I was a kid. We were all smiling. We were a happy, normal-looking trio and I used to imagine a life where we were still that way.

Again, like Dad, I know little of our mum's early life other than she was adopted by an older couple as her birth mother was single. That's it. That's all I know.

Even from a young age I felt losing our mum was tougher for the boys than me.

I had no memory of her. Nothing to compare with the then and now. My brothers knew how she cooked, how she spoke, how she smelled and how she held.

Barry has hardly any memory of his childhood apart from being terrified of Dad, but John, who never talks much about the past as it's 'too bloody maudlin', remembers with great fondness 'a very lovely mummy who was our whole world'.

After Bridget died all the focus was on me as I was the baby and a girl. Fame!

Back in the 1960s there wasn't much known about therapy, and grief counselling certainly wasn't a thing anyone was aware of.

My brothers were ten and eight and from what I can gather they were just expected to get on with it. What a joke.

Joan and Paddy Galvin were part of the community. Joan hailed from working-class Bloomsbury in London and Paddy from Waterford in Ireland. They had four kids, Michael, Sean, Jane and Siobhan. They would later have two more, Liam and Martin, but when they became my 'part-time family' there was just those first four.

They lived in Canonbury Court which was a council-owned, sprawling block of flats across the road from Halton Mansions.

After the Manchester debacle Auntie Joan and Uncle Paddy suggested that they could take care of me up until I went to school and with my real family living so close by I could spend the odd night and weekend back with the boys. Perfect.

I loved the Galvins. Auntie Joan, all long legs and glasses, was a brilliant cook. I've been a vegetarian and eventual pescatarian for nearly forty years now but can still remember the taste of her lovely juicy sausages with homemade chips and delicious lemon meringue pie for pudding. They insisted on good manners and we always had to ask, 'Please may I leave the table?' when a meal was finished. Uncle Paddy, a small man with a distant disposition, was fantastic at DIY. He was always fixing and painting. Thinking of him now, he's up a ladder.

Michael and Sean were great substitute brothers, but Jane and Siobhan were the best pretend sisters a little girl could hope for. They were only a couple of years older than me but, of course, at a tender age they seemed very grown up. Jane was hilarious, always cracking silly jokes and taking the piss (or 'mick' as it was called in their house – no swearing, please!) and Siobhan was just incredibly kind. She always looked out for me.

My cot at home was a ramshackle of cloth and nonsense but at the Galvins' I had a brand-new child's bed in the same room as the girls, who shared a bunk bed. I had lovely striped flannel sheets, woolly blankets and an eiderdown plonked on top.

An abiding memory is of Auntie Joan tucking the sheets in so tightly that I'd sometimes get stuck. As I've said, I was a fitful sleeper and every now and then I'd find myself waking up with my head where my feet should've been, trapped in a tight cocoon of darkness, crying out for help.

Siobhan would always come to my rescue, calling out, 'Mummy! Kathy Burke's got herself stuck again!' while her little hands desperately tried to tug off my suffocating monster.

I was always known by my full name at the Galvins'. Not my *full* full name, which is Katherine Lucy Burke (posh), but Kathy Burke, or Little Kathy Burke, which I liked the best.

Even when very small I must've been fully aware of my situation. Michael Galvin once recalled a particular day when he was around twelve when he picked me up from nursery school after, unbeknown to him, my very first stage appearance.

I was in a production of the children's nursery rhyme 'Sing a Song of Sixpence'. I had a leading role as the bird who pecked off the maid's nose. I can remember our makeshift black wings and beaks and being huddled under whatever it was that represented the pie. As we fluttered out I made my way towards the maid. I think I was meant to just pluck off her nose and fly off but upon seeing the audience I decided to make more of it. Adults would often pretend to pull off a kid's nose by tucking their thumb into their first two fingers then showing it to the gobsmacked child, so I decided to do the same. Nose plucked I then proceeded to show it, thumb tucked, etc. to the front row of adults. I got big laughs so went back along the row again and would've no doubt continued if I hadn't been ushered off by a teacher.

Filing out of nursery with the small chattering crowd, I spotted Michael waiting for me at the gate. He was bemused by what was happening. Why had everybody been inside? What was going on? As he held my hand to take me 'home' I told him all about my leading role and how funny I was and how much I loved it. He stopped us walking, looked down at me and asked why I hadn't told anyone we were doing a show. I looked back up at him and nonchalantly replied, 'Because they told us to tell our mummies.'

FEELING GROOVY

Patricia Cook was a young, happening chick from a working-class background who got herself into university to study child psychology. This was still a pretty rare achievement for a woman in the late 1960s, especially one who grew up in a small terraced house in Wigan, Lancashire.

Long blonde hair, mini skirt and sexy boots, she was friends with my social worker and about to embark on a dissertation looking into the behaviours of very young children without mothers. Particularly girls.

Did my social worker know of anyone under her care who fitted that description?

Well yes, she jolly well did.

An initial meeting was set up with my dad to discuss the situation and he agreed that Pat Cook could take me out on a Sunday afternoon for some ice cream.

I was coming up to four years old. She must've liked me because she continued to take me out at least one Sunday of most months until I was around ten.

We went everywhere and I saw everything. Over the years she took me to most of the museums and art galleries in London. We sometimes went to a Chinese restaurant for lunch. One time we took a black cab somewhere and I thought it was the best thing ever. After that I bothered her constantly about getting a taxi whenever we went out, but she told me that it had been a one-off as they were very expensive. I think this was when my addiction to black cabs started.

If we weren't going on an outing I would spend the day at one of the two rented flats she lived in during the time I knew her. The first was in a house in Mecklenburgh Square in Bloomsbury. The quadrangle of grand Georgian houses surrounded a private garden that you needed a key for, and nearby was Coram's Fields, a famous park by Great Ormond Street Children's Hospital that adults weren't allowed into unless they were with a kid. It's still this way today. I spent hours in both.

Her second flat was in a small private tower block opposite Parliament Hill Fields. It wasn't like the council towers my friends lived in. It was modern, clean and its always-working lifts didn't stink of piss.

Both flats, though very different, were the same in essence. The aroma was real coffee. There were vases of flowers and white shelving filled with books and pieces of art. Best of all, a wardrobe full of Pat's clothes with an abundance of floppy hats, scarves and shoes, which she allowed me to play dress-up with.

Sometimes we would go to other people's houses. Pat had lots of cool, intellectual friends. Doctors, lecturers, sculptors and the like. There were guitars and pianos. One house had a harpsichord, which blew my tiny mind.

She bought me a Che Guevara tee shirt and gave me strawberry yogurts. She told me about feminism and women's rights. She had the first cassette recorder I had ever seen or heard and always had a glass of water by her bed alongside a packet of tiny pills.

When Pat learned to drive and had her own car, I had holidays in the Lake District and a few Christmases with her beautiful family in Wigan. I was treated like one of their own. Her mum and dad, Mr and Mrs Cook, had a grandson Jason, who was Pat's sister Betty's kid. I got the same amount of presents and what felt like the same amount of love. Mrs Cook once made me a giant knitted rabbit and another time a two-piece pink flared trouser suit. Groovy!

One Christmas, Mrs Cook said she was taking me to a pantomime in Manchester for a treat. Just me and her. I'd spotted a poster of *Cinderella*, starring Clodagh Rodgers, who was a famous singer at the time, so hoped we were going to that, but Mrs Cook said no, she'd already booked the tickets for another show, *Robinson Crusoe*, so we wouldn't be seeing Clodagh.

I was outwardly furious. I was the kid so surely I should get to see what I wanted? *Robinson Crusoe????* I didn't want to see a boys' thing, I wanted to see pretty Clodagh Rodgers from *Top of the Pops* as pretty Cinderella!

I grumpily sat down in the stalls of a packed auditorium, determined not to enjoy my little fat spoiled self. The house lights dimmed, a spotlight hit the stage and tumbling from the wings in a series of roly-polies came my hero and comedy superstar of the time, Norman Wisdom.

I cried and, more importantly, felt a wee bit ashamed.

What a twit.

How lucky I was to have these wonderful, kind people in my life.

Aged around six, Pat turned up with a boyfriend called Meir Spungin. Eh?

He had a beard and spoke with a strange accent. He was South African and Jewish. I didn't know what either of those things were.

I was suspicious at first, and of course jealous, but very quickly grew to like him. He was funny and very outspoken, mostly about politics and cricket. He taught me to swim and how to ride the bike they had bought for my tenth birthday – to soften the blow that they were moving to Holland.

Pat converted to Judaism, married Meir and they were starting to have kids of their own. They wanted to try a different life away from London.

We would write.

FREEDOM

Living on the ground floor of Halton Mansions had one great advantage: I could climb out of my bedroom window.

Now permanently home from the Galvins', at five I was more or less left to my own devices.

Mums have radars. They seem to know where kids are. Dads, not so much, especially in the era I grew up in. We had much more freedom back then and it wasn't unusual to see children, even little ones, wandering around the streets unaccompanied.

We had a great park just across the road from us. One area for the oldies with little ponds, rocks and benches, the other a playground with swings, slides and the mighty, unconquered umbrella.

I would always wake up too early. Dad would either be up and out to work by 6 a.m. or snoring like a bear with his mountainous back heaving in the rickety double bed he used to share with our mum.

On warm days I would crack open the bottom of the window and look out at the stillness. One day I thought I could actually climb out. It was only a two-foot drop on to the grassy patch outside. So I did. Upon the realisation that I couldn't hoick myself back in the way I'd come out, I decided to go to the park to kill some time before my brothers woke up.

It was locked so I squeezed myself through the wrought iron bars that made up its fence.

I swung on the swings and hopped on to the little roundabout. I went up and down the baby slide. I went into the rock park and crossed its tiny bridge and talked to my imaginary friends about nothing at all.

When I got hungry I made my way home. On tippy-toes I flicked the letter box as best I could as I was unable to reach the knocker.

After what felt like an eternity, a bleary-eyed John opened the door and was shocked to find me there.

I entered and walked down our dark passageway towards the front room that led into a small kitchen, passing John and Barry's room, bathroom and coal cupboard to the right, mine and Dad's shared room to the left.

As John fixed me some cornflakes I proceeded to tell him all about my adventure. He said I was still too little to be wandering around on my own and that I wasn't to do it again.

But I did. Many times.

Our front door was directly opposite our neighbours, Mrs and Miss Baynham. Mrs Baynham seemed very old to me at the time but was probably only in her fifties, and her daughter, Miss Baynham, was about twenty years younger. They were lovely and would often invite us into their flat to take a couple of sweets from a crystal jar that lived inside a sideboard from the 1920s. Their neat flat was always quiet, a ticking clock being the only sound I can remember.

Miss Baynham was known as a spinster.

One morning they caught me sitting on the bottom step of the block staircase, waiting for our door to be answered and they were not happy.

Poor John got a telling-off even though he'd told me count-less times I was being naughty.

I just couldn't help myself. I loved my early-morning, solitary rambles.

The solution? I was given my own key for my sixth birthday and a milk crate was put outside the door so I could reach the lock and no longer wake everyone up with my knocking.

GO STAND IN THE CORNER!

Primary school was a hoot, up to a point. Some of the teachers were strict and I had a whack round the back of my legs with the ruler quite a few times, but on the whole I liked being there.

One day a new girl arrived with ringlets in her hair. She was screaming the place down as she didn't want her mummy to leave her. It was all a bit much so her mum took her home and tried again the following day. Again, screams, tears and tortured cries of 'Don't leave me, Mummy!' I thought this was all a bit dramatic and decided to intervene. I went over to the kicking and screaming ball of mess, told her my name and said very matter-of-factly that my mummy was *dead* and that I would never see her again, but she would see her mummy at the end of the day. Shocked silence. I held out my hand, she took it and let me lead her into the classroom.

My new best friend Diane and I were very naughty together. Anything could set us off laughing so we were constantly sent to different corners of the classroom to face the wall. If we took a quick glance at each other this could set us off again with shoulders shaking and happy tears streaming.

We were known by our respective parents as a 'pair of fecking eejits'.

Our gang of pals were Bernice, Claire, Sandra, Marcella and Esther. We still meet up now about once a year for a ladies' lunch and to reminisce. We all agree that Claire's birthday parties were the best. Her lovely mum and dad were lower middle class as they were teachers but to me they seemed posh. They had a piano and my favourite food there was Claire's mum's eggy

19

bread, although she did tell me once that she was very sorry but she couldn't always afford to give me eggy bread and even though they were teachers it didn't mean they were rich. I didn't believe her.

Life at home could be a challenge but myself and my brothers never told any grown-ups about our dad's erratic and often violent behaviour. I was just naughty and constantly seeking attention and affirmation from my classmates. I wonder how many other 'class clowns' were covering up a deep-rooted unhappiness? Millions, I bet. And millions more to come.

We had a few of the usual day trips away from school, which were always good fun. Hampton Court, London Zoo and, my favourite, the Tower of London. I loved the gruesomeness of the torture chambers and beheading blocks.

In our last year we had a trip to Calais. Setting off at the crack of dawn to wander around on foreign turf for what felt like five minutes before heading back home on the ferry, clutching miniature Eiffel Towers.

A girl in our class, Camilla, was without a partner for that trip so Diane and I said she could team up with us. Di wasn't as rough and tumble as me but Camilla was. The crossing back home was pretty choppy but she and I had a blast up on deck, laughing our heads off while getting thrown about by the waves and drenched by the spray from the English Channel.

Some of the kids' mums were chaperoning and I remember staring at a tough boy called Raymond who was snuggled into his mum's lap with feelings of seasickness. So strange to see him being coddled like that. I didn't miss my mum as I never knew her but that was the first time I remember missing *having* a mum.

The school had a lovely headteacher, Sister Joan. I remember her being very smiley and if she saw me in the playground she'd always give me a little cwtch (she wasn't Welsh, I just find their word for cuddle more apt). Disaster struck before our final year, though, as she'd fallen in love and was leaving the nunnery and school to get married. Good for her. She was beautiful and deserved happiness but her replacement was a rotten old bitch who didn't seem to like kids – especially me. Our last year included taking the Catholic confirmation. This is where you're confirmed into the Catholic Church as an adult. The best part about it was choosing a saint's name to officially add to your own name. We had to do some extra lessons after school in preparation. I can't remember what exactly was going on at home at the time but it included having to be back to do certain chores, causing me to miss a couple of classes. There wasn't an inch of understanding let alone sympathy from the head when she called me into her office to explain my absence. I probably didn't tell her the whole truth of our situation, but she would've known that a mum wasn't around. She told me I was wicked and lazy and as punishment I wouldn't be allowed to take my confirmation along with my peers. I cried my heart out. Not bothered as much about the situation itself as how my dad would react. It would be my fault whatever and I knew a few punches to my head would be on the cards. And so it was.

I finally made my confirmation a few years later under Auntie Joan Galvin's insistence. There I was, aged fifteen, with her son Liam and a big gang of 12-year-olds, me wearing a skirt and frilly blouse with my skinhead haircut on top. I was more than a little embarrassed but at least now I had my chosen saint's name added to my others, which was Bridget.

THE ISLINGTON ELITE

Yes I am and always have been.

Halton Mansions lies bang in the middle of Upper Street and Essex Road, two of Islington's main streets that meet in the middle at Islington Green. Follow Islington High Street up from the green and at the top you'll find The Angel and its Tube station.

This whole area was and still is my stomping ground.

I went to St John Evangelist primary school, where my brothers had been taught, along with the Galvin children and Nellie and Denny's kids Mary, Denise, Robert and, a bit later, Angela.

Most of the wider Irish community in the area went there, along with the Greeks, Italians, Jamaicans, etc. A big old melting pot, all with one thing in common: Catholicism.

St John's and its adjoining church are situated in the heart of The Angel, about a twenty-minute saunter from the flats. By the time I was home permanently, John and Barry had already started secondary school so one of the Galvin kids would walk with me or, a bit later, an older girl called Mary Riley would have the honour.

John and Barry had got into the best secondary Catholic boys' school in town, the London Oratory, which was on the Brompton Road in Fulham. *Fulham?!* Five miles from home. There and back, every single day. What bright spark came up with that idea? It's very impressive that they were clever enough to get in but really? Two boys who had lost their mum and were expected to do cooking and cleaning as well as looking after a snotty little girl?

Surely a school closer to home would have been more appropriate?

John would get me up, make breakfast then walk me to the Rileys' before embarking on the long journey to his school. Then, when we were home, he'd cook the tea and he and Barry would share the chores. When I got bigger, from around seven or eight I think, I too would do some chores. I honestly don't remember our dad doing much. Sure, he sometimes went to work all day but his sporadic boozing meant this wasn't always the case. John recalls that on the day I officially left the Galvins' he and Dad carried my small but heavy bed from their flat to ours. A flurry of snow had started to fall. By the time they arrived, old cot dumped by the bin chutes and new bed placed into Dad's room by the window, the weather had become atrocious.

And Dad sent John out to get us all some chips. What a guy!

The owner of the chippy stated to the queue of customers in his thick Greek accent, 'This isn't London snow, this is Siberian snow!'

John stuffed the packets of chips inside his coat in a desperate attempt to keep them warm, knowing he'd be shouted at if they arrived cold despite the uncontrollable elements.

Islington has always had its 'posh bits'. Grand houses homing judges, lawyers and the like sit alongside the council blocks.

Camden Passage, which runs parallel with Islington High Street, was full of antique shops and stalls selling little vintage items. It opened Wednesdays and Saturdays. On Wednesdays, walking through it on the way home from school, I used to pretend I was a posh person and bother the shopkeepers with a terrible over-the-top posh accent asking about 'lamps for the nanny's room'. Some would humour me but most would just roll their eyes and ask politely for me to leave. One time, a red-faced man with an incredibly plummy voice told me to 'Fuck orf!' which made me laugh so much I weed.

My favourite place in Camden Passage and indeed the whole of Islington was the Angel Bookshop. Sadly no longer there. I couldn't afford to buy anything, we got all our books from the Essex Road library, but the people who ran it would let me sit on its creaky steps by the children's section and, as long as my hands were clean, I could stay skimming through the pages of its latest offerings for as long as I liked, quietly farting all the while as the smell of the books put me into a state of relaxation. Astérix was a particular favourite.

I loved reading. It was the only thing I was any good at, apart from swimming once I'd learned. I started to read the *Daily Mirror* from when I was around seven, and John and Barry would pass on any books they'd enjoyed, hence my love of 'boys' books' rather than the girlie ones.

Whenever there was a primary school nativity I would be one of the readers, always! I never got a chance to perform. I was even told by a very stupid person that I wasn't pretty enough to be Mary and that my reading was excellent so I should be grateful to be given such an important job. I thought portraying the mother of Jesus was the most important job, but hey-ho.

I would also pass the time in the aforementioned Essex Road library. It had a fantastic children's and young adults' room and a quieter, much bigger adults-only room. It had a grand staircase that led to a large hall where we would see puppet shows and films made by the Children's Film Foundation and buy orange squash and sandwiches for a teeny-tiny fee.

I was given access to the adults' library room earlier than most of my peers because my reading was so advanced, but they kept an eye on what I was taking out, making sure the books were appropriate. No Alan Sillitoe for me just yet.

My favourite book as a kid, though, was our Family Allowance benefit book. When Dad was on a binge, money was tighter than usual so we relied on our extra benefits. I loved that book. I loved going to the post office with Barry to get it stamped and seeing the money being passed through the hatch.

I felt a lot of kindness for our situation from Islington Council. We weren't the only ones on the poverty line and I don't recall us ever being made to feel ashamed. Free school meals were fantastic as far as I was concerned, and if we were hungry during the school holidays there were plenty of places to fill ourselves up, my favourite being the Union Chapel on Upper Street. This huge Gothic-style building is now known as a music venue but you can also hire rooms for meetings and the like. I've used a couple of its spaces to rehearse some of the plays I've directed during my adult years. The smell of cooking would waft through the building at midday because it's still providing food for the homeless and those in need.

I hate today's rhetoric of looking down on people on bene-fits – all the fault of the Murdoch and Rothermere press barons, of course. Those scumbags love to set the working classes against each other. All that fucking money, and stirring hate is what they choose to do with it? How utterly pathetic.

The only time I remember being angry with the council was when the ABC Cinema on Essex Road was turned into a Mecca bingo hall. I loved going to Saturday morning pictures with John and Barry, when we could afford to, and was heartbroken at the change. The oldies had pubs so why the flip did they need a flipping bingo hall?!

Another favourite but long-gone place of my childhood was the swimming pool, known locally as Tibs because it was situated on Tibberton Square. It's where our primary school went for swimming but try as I might, I couldn't get to grips with it with our teachers, but when Meir Spungin came into my life he somehow managed to get me going without the dreaded floater boards. Maybe it was the undivided attention?

Once I started I was unstoppable and went to Tibs as often as funds permitted, making sure there was enough money to include a chip butty for the short walk home.

By the time I got to my pre-teens I was an excellent swimmer. Speciality the backstroke. I could also, after much determined practice, swim a whole length underwater.

A lifeguard called Betty noticed my skills and took me under her wing for a bit. She had peroxide-blonde hair, a lovely figure and always wore white. I went to her flat in one of the mansion blocks on Upper Street for squash and cake. She talked to my dad about training and what would be required.

Nothing came of it, though. On a day out with the Corcorans to Canvey Island a wobbly kettle over a camper stove put an end to my sporting career by suddenly tipping and spilling its boiling fullness on to my leg, rendering me swim-free for six weeks. This, combined with learning that I would have to train before school, put my Olympic dream to bed.

Betty was lovely, though, and I was sad to disappoint her.

I became a member of the Islington Boat Club when I was around twelve years old. By then I was babysitting so had my own money for membership. I remember canoeing on the still waters at the Angel end of Regent's Canal on peaceful Sunday afternoons. I loved the life jackets and the hot chocolate afterwards. It was also where a boy tried to kiss me for the first time – but I declined through fear and disbelief.

Youth clubs, the fair coming to Highbury Fields, whizzing around the flats on roller skates or having bike races around an empty Highbury roundabout on Sunday mornings, there was always so much to do. So much fun to be had. And I grabbed every opportunity to have it.

FOUR CANDLES

The miners' strikes of the early 1970s caused three-day weeks and blackouts, which for a kid like me was fantastic.

Dad decided I might be a bit much for John and Barry to look after during all this (sense at last!) so I was to stay with the Corcorans at their cosy council flat in Highbury until the strikes were over.

I loved hunkering down with Mary and Denise in their room. Like the Galvin girls, they were a bit older and to me were the coolest people ever. They had posters of The Osmonds but their big obsession was David Cassidy. He was a dreamboat. Mary even went to see him in concert, which was massive as Cassidy mania was all over the news. She came back disappointed, though, as the noise from the screaming fans had drowned out his singing.

I loved having Auntie Nellie's food on the regular, the lid lifting on the spitting pressure cooker to reveal something delicious most evenings. Her stews were magnificent, especially when served with her buttery mashed potatoes and swede. The Corcorans weren't big drinkers but Nellie and Denny would have a small glass of white wine with their Sunday roast.

We always had to say our prayers before food and the lead-up to bedtime involved doing the rosary, which for me lasted an eternity. But their soft whispered chanting did feel extra special by candlelight and my sleeping was immensely improved.

I remember Mary's and Denise's beds shaking with laughter when they asked what I wanted to be when I grew up. I unashamedly replied, 'A striptease artist!' Where in the hell had I got that notion from? Gawd knows. I should imagine it was from old black and white movies that were constantly on the telly. Those ladies were extremely glamorous. Plus, I once did an impromptu strip-down to my knickers for a couple of boys behind the school toilet block for which they paid me in Black Jack and Fruit Salad sweeties. It made me feel quite powerful.

KERRR-CHING!

I was obsessed with money as a kid. Knowing my striptease efforts couldn't be relied upon, I had to find a new way to get my own cash. I was given money for birthdays and Christmas every now and then but, like most kids of my generation, pocket money wasn't really a thing. I nicked a lot of money from my dad. One of the upsides of him being in a drunken sleep was me being able to stick my fingers into his trouser pockets, scooping out coins while he spluttered in his armchair.

I would also keep any bus fare money and walk wherever I needed to be. I loved walking so it was no hardship and the kids' fare at that time cost the same amount as a packet of crisps. Walk, crunch, walk, crunch. Lovely.

During the six-week summer holidays, John and, when he was old enough, Barry would work with Dad on the building sites. This was a magical time. We always had proper dinners, made by John after a hard day's graft. Sausages and mash, steak and kidney stew or liver and bacon. So much better than our regular diet of tinned soup with boiled spuds. John had been taught to cook by a couple of home helps who were assigned after Mum died. Once he realised Dad's cooking was pretty bad, John asked them to teach him a few basic things. He was brilliant. I can't remember not liking anything he served up.

Not only was there better food on the table, but John had saved up and bought a stereo system. Amazing. The Beatles and David Bowie were a constant, and comedies like *Round the Horne* seemed funnier coming through the speakers.

We once won on the football pools. Forty-seven pounds,

which was a fortune. Dad gave us a fiver from the winnings, bought whatever was needed for the flat and disappeared for the weekend with the rest. John got us a massive punnet of strawberries and a huge tub of real cream and we sprinkled a ton of sugar on top. I was blissfully sick afterwards.

I was around ten years old when I got my first job babysitting. I was playing out on the grass in front of the flats when Molly approached me. She had three kids all under eight and I was deemed responsible enough to look after them. I loved Molly. She was Irish – I can't remember where from exactly – and smoked like a chimney. She had mental health problems, but I was unaware of how bad they were. She was always kind and very funny. Her laugh was a rasping smoker's and her eyes would fill with happy tears, her pretty, round face catching them on rosy-apple cheeks. She constantly rolled pinches of white bread into little balls of grey. You'd find them all over her flat. I can't remember exactly how much I was paid to look after her kids, but I do remember that delicious feeling of having my own money that nobody else could touch. I'd buy bars of chocolate and eventually saved enough to get my roller skates. If Molly was short on cash, though, she'd pay me in cigarettes. We'd sit together and smoke while we listened and sang along to a Max Bygraves record. Which I liked the best.

The blocks in Halton Mansions were all open in those days. You could whizz about the place and zoom in and out of the blocks. Brilliant for 'knock down ginger' and hide-and-seek.

What wasn't so brilliant was they were a hunting ground for 'dirty old men' or 'flashers'. You'd often come across one lurking, ready to expose themselves to some unsuspecting kid. We'd just point and laugh at them until they shuffled off, humiliated.

Sometimes I'd search the blocks for coins. This was particularly successful on Sunday mornings, if I got out early enough. Pissed adults on a Saturday night reaching home after the pub, searching for keys in trouser pockets or handbags would drop coins in the scramble and couldn't be arsed to search for the rolled-away ones. It was an easy job.

Molly was also responsible for me getting my first cat. Her cat had kittens and I persuaded Dad to let me take one. I called him Nobby. Dad found this name uncouth so would call him Nobert instead. Nobby was a wild one who would spit, hiss and scratch anyone who went near him except me. We once had a knock on our front door very late at night from a neighbour in a nearby block who couldn't get into their flat as Nobby had parked himself on their doormat and wouldn't budge. They'd thrown water at him and poked him with a broom handle to no avail. I arrived with a blanket to find a small crowd of people staring at this very aggressive creature who was now making the most awful guttural sounds. I apologised, said he'd had a hard life, which got a nervous laugh from some, threw the blanket over him then scooped it, twisted the ends turning it into a makeshift sack, threw it and him over my shoulder and headed off back to ours like a hero wrangler.

BROTHERS

John and Barry were and are very different. John is outgoing, gregarious and funny in a silly 'dad jokes' way, Barry is shy with a quick wit but he's a man of few words. I'm a mix of both. John is small in stature with glasses, Barry a bit more heavy-set and again, I'm a mix of both.

John was always into art; Barry, sport. Shared loves, though, were taking the piss out of Dad, when he wasn't around of course, and music and comedy. Old repeats of The Goons or Kenny Everett on the radio, Morecambe and Wise and Dave Allen on TV. They also liked 'brainy' programmes like documentaries and the series *The Ascent of Man*. I found these dull and mostly incomprehensible, but I did love watching *Play for Today*.

John was the boss. He ran the house. Setting chores for myself and Barry, trying to keep everything shipshape. Our living room was quite sparse compared to my friends' homes. There were no knick-knacks or pictures on the walls, just a couple of photos on the mantelpiece of us as littler kids, so not much dusting was needed, but the weekly routine of shopping, laundrette visiting, fetching coal from the coal yard near the library and mopping the linoleum floors was stuck to like clockwork.

When money was tight, which felt like *all* of the time, Bill who owned the corner shop across the road would give us stuff on tick. It would be left to John to do the asking as Bill wasn't keen on Dad but really liked and missed our mum who used to clean for him. John would also be sent to the Galvins or Corcorans for handouts and never left empty-handed.

Barry would sometimes go to the Arsenal Stadium to watch

his favourite footie team. It was 'his thing' and not to be shared. After a while, though, John got curious and asked Barry if he could tag along to a match, paying his own way of course. Barry reluctantly agreed but warned John that as they were to be situated in the North Bank it could get extremely rowdy and sometimes aggressive, but this didn't put John off.

When they returned, Barry was furious and constantly shook his head in disbelief. 'We could've got our fucking heads kicked in!' John had apparently found the match 'extremely boring' so took a book from his pocket and started to read instead.

No doubt a fight then took place between them. I can't remember if that was specifically the case as there were many fights. Sometimes I jumped in, trying to stop them, but more often than not I'd just get caught up in it. Slapping, punching, pinching and kicking. We all went for it. My speciality was hair pulling.

One time, John was at one end of our dark hallway, Barry at the other and weapons were being thrown. I stuck my head out from my bedroom door to have a nose when – chaos! A knife that had been hurtled through the air was now, in slow motion, spinning its way towards me through the gloom then landing and subsequently slicing into my bottom lip. I didn't like getting the stitches for it but I did enjoy the attention and the lipstick of ointment I had to regularly use once the stitches were taken out. It made me feel like a teenager.

Barry and I once had a secret pet white mouse called Dennis. Barry had bought him from a pet shop on the Essex Road and he lived in an old school desk in John and Barry's bedroom. We'd get him out from his hiding place and let him scamper over us, disappearing up one sleeve and popping out from the other. Still to this day John doesn't believe this happened as how could he not know about it? But it was true. Poor Dennis only lived a couple of days, though, as he'd gnawed into something unpalatable and subsequently pegged it. I was terribly upset and said we should bury him or at least give him some sort of funeral. We went outside to the patch of green where a tree lived and Barry unceremoniously took Dennis's stiff corpse and hurled him high into the branches, declaring, 'The birds can have him, it's nature's way!'

The boys never seemed to be included in the fun I was having outside the house, although they did once come with me to Pat Cook's for a Sunday lunch. I loved showing them her flat, 'Look, fitted carpets! Look, this is apple juice!' They had their own friends of course but I always felt a pang of guilt whenever I went off for a special day out without them.

Over a couple of summers we were sent to Devon for a break with a farming family who took in kids through social services. I sort of liked it but much preferred my urban life with its freedom and lack of care. The boys seemed to love it, though. I can still see Barry running through the farm's fields, trying to help the owner catch some escaped chicks. I'd never seen him laugh so much. I think John benefited the most. What a welcome break from shopping, cleaning and cooking it must've been. He'd take himself off most days with a large drawing pad and some watercolours and come back in time for tea, sun-kissed and happy with his day's work.

A nearby farm had a large barn that would have dances and one particular time before the dance there was to be a kids' painting competition. I encouraged John to enter. He came second to the daughter of the owner of the barn whose work was obviously crap. So I said so. Actually I went fucking mad, crying out at the injustice. I got a slapped leg from Mrs Farmer, sent back to where we were staying and ordered to go straight to bed. John quietly tapped on my bedroom door when they returned later that night. He entered, gave me a packet of crisps he'd filched from the kitchen and said I was a silly little cow for showing him up but I was right, the girl's painting *was* crap. Justified!

Along with mimicking Dad's accent, John and Barry were also great at copying our favourite comedy stars from the radio and TV and I would copy the boys. I loved making them laugh but sometimes this was unintentional. Whenever I returned from my Wigan trips with Pat Cook the boys would find it hilarious that I'd picked up the accent. In I'd come, full of 'thee's and 'eeh's and they'd roll about, holding their tummies with tears in their eyes and asking, where had I left my whippet?

When Barry was around fourteen he got a Saturday job working at Lipton's supermarket. This was a great time as there were always discounts or about-to-turn stuff that the staff could take. I loved the sudden abundance of sliced bacon that John would put into thick-cut slices of bread with loads of butter and spicy brown sauce.

When the boys got into their late teenage years I saw less of them. Things still got done in the home but every opportunity they could spend outside of it was taken. And the same went for me.

A KINDNESS

Chores I hated doing were cleaning the kitchen and the bathroom, taking the rubbish out to the bin chutes and going to the laundrette as it was really fucking dull. A favourite chore was getting up early on a Saturday morning to fetch the freshly baked bread from the bakery on Essex Road. However, Dad put a stop to me having this job because I'd pick away at the heel of the loaf on my way home; dawdling, picking and chomping in my own little piggy world. It was just too warm and delicious to resist, so I was sacked.

A job I used to hate but started to like was getting the veg for the weekend. Our list never changed: potatoes, onions, carrots and cabbage – and if there was any extra money, apples were added. The bag weighed a ton, and I'd get bruises on my shins from it knocking against my legs. A young man from the flats opened a fruit and veg stall on Greenman Street and John noticed that he was a bit cheaper than our usual place, so I was sent there instead. We didn't know him, maybe the brothers knew him to nod at but he wasn't a friend they talked about. But he seemed to know us – probably because of losing our mum – and sometimes he'd put extra stuff in the bag for free. In the winter, he'd chuck in some parsnips and swede, and in the summer months I'd come home with added oranges and plums. He never said anything more than 'Hello kid, how are you doing?' And then he'd proceed to add the extra goodies. This went on for years, until one Saturday he wasn't there any more, and the new stall owner didn't bother with a greeting and just gave me what was on my list. Gutted.

Cut to my adult life and I'm in a black cab (my preferred mode of transport) when I asked the cabbie – 'Excuse me, do I know you from somewhere?'

He smiled and said yes, he was Dave and he used to be a greengrocer when I was a kid. Happy tears sprang at the memory of this man's kindness.

'You were so lovely to me,' I said. 'Your kindness made a huge impact on my life.'

He laughed and said, 'Glad to hear it! My way of thinking is, if you're nice to people then hopefully they'll be nice to others.' So I was. I'm a generous tipper – but Dave got the biggest tip ever.

DRUNK I

Life was sometimes strangely easier when Dad was drinking as he was hardly home. John once told me, when I brought up the question of how did he and Barry feel when I went off for my Christmas holidays with Pat Cook, that it was actually great because not only was I not around to look after and worry about but Dad was also absent. He'd leave the boys, then in their early teens, some money, tell them to get on with it and disappear for the duration. Peace to all men.

On the odd occasion through my childhood Dad would bring a couple of pals home with him, mainly if they had bought extra booze from an off-licence and needed somewhere warm to neck it. They were never horrible people and Dad's mood was always brighter in their company. For years I was under the impression that the great actor Peter O'Toole was once present. I remember a well-spoken man, dressed in a finery that was unusual for Dad's friends, talking to me about being an actor as even as a little kid I'd probably expressed this was what I wanted to be. Later, when I brought this up with John he said I was being ridiculous, there was no way Peter O'Toole had ever been in our scruffy little flat. Then a few minutes later he said, 'I think it was Richard Harris.'

Dad's girlfriends were interesting. I never knew their names and they only appeared once in a blue moon during the night. I'd sometimes wake up to see some woman asleep in the bed with Dad but by the morning she'd be gone. I spied one particular lady sitting on the edge of his bed facing mine, injecting herself. Dad was snoring away so I plucked up the courage to whisper, 'Hello, what you doing?'

She was a bit startled but whispered back, 'I'm just taking my medicine, darling, you go back to sleep.' I pretended to close my eyes but kept peeking as she took a strap off her arm, stuffed the paraphernalia into a bag, lay back down on the bed and was eventually breathing in time with Dad. She too was gone by the morning.

Some of the time when Dad was drunk his mood was upbeat. He'd sit in his armchair whistling tunelessly and express feelings of love for us all, but if he'd had a bothersome night of arguing in the pub or the street he'd crash into the bedrooms, screaming blue murder about how we were ungrateful cunts who needed a good hiding. The boys got this more than me. Prick. With me he'd cry crocodile tears about how much he missed my mum and how lonely he was and could he have a cuddle? I'd be as stiff as a board in his arms, the smell of cheap whisky knocking me sick waiting for him to pass out, which luckily would happen quite quickly.

My favourite thing to do while he slept in his chair was to gently comb his Brylcreemed hair into a slick side parting, get a dab of black soot from the fireplace to put under his nose and start goose-stepping around the room, whispering 'Sieg heil, mein Führer!' His drunken rages could be terrifying, though. The worst times being if his money ran out and he was home early. He'd sway around in the kitchen looking for food, giving out about us eating everything. John would take terrible risks with his piss taking. He'd put on a posh voice and pretend to smoke a pipe. 'We're awfully sorry, Pater, for eating the last of the pheasant, maybe there's a little caviar at the back of the fridge?'

Dad's eyes would go lime green with anger. 'Don't you take the piss out of me! It's my name on the fecking rent book!!!'

He had a few nights in the cells for being drunk and disorderly. A nice policeman would come and tell us where he was in case we were worried (we weren't). And a few nights were spent in the hospital either from fighting or falling over. One Christmastime, when I was a teenager, he fell down some concrete steps and cracked his head open. I went to visit him. Off his head on painkillers, he was laughing away as he thought it was hilarious that a Santa had been on a ward round and given him a washbag as a gift, exclaiming, 'That's the first fecking present I've had from Father Christmas in my life!'

'Lucky you,' I replied dryly, 'I got fuck-all.' Which made him laugh even harder.

FAT AND UGLY

I was always fat-looking, though not always fat, my double chin giving the impression of more meat on the bones than there sometimes was. Auntie Joan once said, 'You got exactly the same amount of food as my own kids so gawd knows why you were chubby.' Genetics maybe? Comfort? More likely, though, it was greed. I may have been given the same amount of food as the Galvin kids at mealtimes but it didn't stop me pilfering whatever I came across the rest of the day. I always had second helpings at school and would often hang around at friends' houses until their teatime, when inevitably I'd be asked by the mum if I wanted something. *Oh yes please, Mrs So-and-So!* Then I'd go home to another cooked meal from John.

When Mary Riley was walking with me to primary school, John would make me breakfast then get me to her house on Essex Road by 7.30 a.m., before schlepping his way to Fulham. Mary was a bugger for staying in bed, with her mum constantly shouting up the stairs for her to 'Get up!' The waiting would make me hungry and if Mrs Riley offered some toast or, better still, cereal with hot milk then I of course never refused.

One morning, though, she told John she wanted a word with him. 'Now listen to me, John. I know you've a lot on your plate and it's only a ten-minute walk from yours to here but you *must* give that child something to eat before you leave the house, especially on these cold mornings.'

John said nothing but the look he gave me made my floodgates burst: 'He does give me breakfast!' I wailed. 'But I like Weetabix with hot milk and he don't have time to boil it!'

Mrs R tut-tutted, John rolled his eyes and that was the end of my two breakfasts scandal.

I remember Pat Cook giving me a bath in her lovely mum and dad's house in Wigan and as she was washing my hair she commented on how fine it was. 'I've got thick hair,' she said, 'but yours is thin.'

I found this a bit confusing, as I was known as fat so how could my hair be thin? 'Mine's thick too!' I insisted.

I'd love to have been blessed with fat hair.

'Fat cow' was an insult I was used to from my peers, but the first time I was called 'ugly' was from a grown-up. The ice cream van was parked at the gate of the flats, the usual queue of kids forming a multicoloured snake, with their necks craned while us stragglers with no money would hover enviously. A cockney woman who I'd never seen before suddenly appeared, 'I've had a win on the bingo! Who wants an ice cream?!'

'Me please!' we screamed in unison with hands up in the air. We couldn't believe it.

I was so delighted, I beamed at her with all my might when she said, 'Ooh, ain't you ugly!'

My world stopped while the other kids laughed. I felt awful. I was hurt. It was a feeling I hadn't had before. It made me feel ashamed. What was I supposed to do with that? I held back the tears, swallowed down the lump in my throat, laughed along and replied, 'I'm the best dancer at the ugly bug ball, though!' Then pulled a face and did a little jiggle, which made her laugh and the kids laugh even more.

When she handed me my ice cream, 'I'll have a screwball please, mrs', she apologised, 'Sorry I said you were ugly, love.'

'That's alright,' I said, even though it wasn't.

NAUGHTY

I must've been a nightmare to handle. Not only did I disappear for hours on end causing worry and upset but when I *was* around, misbehaving seemed to be a hobby.

I did the usual naughty things a kid does, talking in class, talking in Mass, talking over adult conversations, but it always felt like I was naughtier than most. I was constantly told to, 'Stop being so bold!'

Nicking money out of Dad's pocket was relatively easy when he was pissed but his dry times meant I was more skint than usual. One morning there was a sixpence piece on the mantel. I remember staring at it for ages. I knew it was there for a reason. John had chronic asthma and Barry was starting to have epileptic fits, or seizures as they're now called. The money was obviously for fares to a hospital appointment for one of the boys. But somehow I convinced myself it was there for me. So I took it.

It was a great day. I bought a couple of large chocolate bars and showed them off to my pals during break time. 'Look what I've got!' *Ooh*, came the response. 'I can share them out with everybody!' *Ooh, thanks Kath!*

I was a queen and a great friend and everyone loved me – but my buzz was killed the minute I got home. Dad went ballistic. What was I thinking?! Searching for a reason, I whimpered I thought it was my pocket money. Pocket money? We never had pocket money so why the feck would I think that? His massive hands picked me up by the scruff and tried with all their might to shake some sense into me, before sending me straight to bed with no TV and no dinner.

I was beside myself. The agony of it! The brothers were amused and no doubt delighted that the dreaded hospital visit had been postponed. I curled up in bed, the sun still bright outside. *I don't care*, I told myself, *I've got my new* Tintin *from the library*. Then, as if he'd read my mind, in stomped the master, whipping my one solace away from my thieving little mitts. 'And no fecking books!'

TEETH

My teeth were always a problem. Not surprising really as my
favourite things to eat were sweets and if they weren't available
a couple of spoons of sugar nicked from the bag that lived in
our very large, very empty, built-in kitchen cupboard could sort
my daily fix. One tooth was a different colour from the rest and
they grew in various sizes. Think Emma Thompson's Nanny
McPhee but 4 foot and less attractive.

I, like most kids, hated the dentist but the bonus of a departed
mum and drinkie dad was no one to check if I went to the
appointments. Which I didn't. Until that is, groovy Pat Cook
came on the scene. She was very worried about my skewwhiff
choppers and the next thing I knew she was gently leading me
by the hand up a mountain of steps that led into the dreaded
Eastman Dental Hospital on Gray's Inn Road.

Fuck me, I hated that place. The reception was large but warm
with brown leather sofas and armchairs. It had the biggest fish
tank I'd ever seen. Lovely little multicoloured creatures swimming
around happily in its tranquil, bubbly atmosphere. So peaceful
and tranquil it lulled me into the worst false sense of security
because upstairs was a horror show. You could hear the screams
from the corridor. An ominous room cut into cubicles welcomed
me. Bright lights beamed into them, casting repulsive shadows
of sadistic monsters against their frosted green glass. What in the
living hell was this??? I thought Pat liked me! I sat squirming
in an over-large slippery chair, mouth open while the monsters
prodded, poked, pinched and stung at my sad unhealthy gums.
Then what looked like a toilet plunger was put over my entire

face and gaseous fumes making me gag engulfed my little system. Blackout.

The stitches in my mouth felt like leggy spiders. I'd constantly run my tongue over them. Bits of food would get stuck so I'd have to rinse with salt water at the end of each day, which made me gag. I couldn't wait to have them removed. But be careful what you wish for. The snipping was more painful and horrible as I was wide awake. Where was the gas when you needed it?!

I think I was about nine when I had a week in Great Ormond Street Hospital. More teeth had appeared in my already crammed gums so they had to be removed. What a wee freak. I liked the hospital. Dad was having a dry spell so visited often and I liked chatting away to the girl in the bed next to me. Her handsome dad was in the army and had his uniform on when he visited, which I thought was very cool. I whispered to her that night that I'd like to marry him. This made her furious, 'I'm not like you!' she hissed. 'I've got a mum!' Alright, mate, I was only trying to be nice. Blimey.

Soon after, I was fitted with a removable plastic plate that was to keep everything in line before I had more procedures. I had to wear it all the time, especially at night. I kept it clean and was quite proud of it as it was pretty unusual for a kid of my age to have one back then. At school I would show off after lunch, proclaiming, 'I have to rinse me plate out!' But then a boy in my class told me he knew someone who choked to death in their sleep because the plate had loosened and slipped down their throat. What?! That night, after cleaning it before bed, I decided it couldn't do any harm to just leave it on the side and I'd put it back on in the morning. It was more of a struggle getting it on the next day, though. It felt a bit tight and the little wiry bits were cutting into my gums but no worries, so I did the same the following night. Disaster! This time the stupid thing had completely shrunk overnight. I couldn't get it back in! Flip, flip, flip! What to do?

So I did nothing. Pat Cook was now Pat Spungin and living in Holland so nobody asked about it. Appointment letters were ignored and the shrivelled plate was chucked in the bin. I wouldn't visit a dentist again until I was in my mid-twenties. Happy days.

WHO WAS THAT?

I couldn't open canned soup. The butterfly wings on the opener were too stiff for my little fingers. If Mrs or Miss Baynham from next door were home they would do it for me but sometimes they weren't.

One time, a lady I didn't know with a high beehive hairdo and rock and roll clothes was putting her rubbish into the bin stores out the back so I approached her with my tin and asked if she could open it for me please. She asked my name and when I told her, said, 'Oh, you're that little girl without a mummy, [fame!] come with me and I'll sort you out with something better than that.' So I did. She lived on the third floor of the row of blocks that looked out over the park. Her flat was clean and full of doilies. They covered the arms and backs of the sofa and chairs and were under ornaments on top of a highly polished glass cabinet. She had a little white poodle dog that I was scared of and she made me the best bacon sandwich I'd ever had.

Another time a younger woman with hair down to her bum who lived further down our row on the ground floor opened her door suddenly when I was running in and out of the blocks. She asked if I could go to the shop for her as she was poorly and I could get myself some sweets with the change. Sure. No problem, guy. When I brought the shopping back — bread, marg, milk and fags — she invited me in.

It was dark. All the curtains were drawn. There was hippy stuff on the walls and floors and something didn't half pong. Joss sticks. My first taste of fake India. She offered me some tea and toast and I sat on a low sofa, chomping happily. I liked her, so the following week I knocked and volunteered to get her shopping again. 'Cool,' she said. But when I returned she didn't invite me in so I asked if I could have a glass of water.

'Okay,' she said, 'but you can't stay because I've got guests.'

'That's okay,' I replied, 'I've got shopping for other people to get.' Which was a lie. She led me down the dark passage into the front room. There were two beardy men sitting on the low sofa smoking *huge* roll-ups. One said hello, the other was a bit sleepy. I drank the water slowly, staring at them while the sleepy one stared back.

I returned one more time. This time the lady was by herself and made me some beans on toast and a mug of tea. We chatted about The Beatles and I told her I was in love with Paul. Then, *bang, bang, bang!* The knock was so loud I jumped and spilled some beans on my trousers. She went down the dark passageway and opened the door. From where I was sitting I could tell the angry, male tones were coming from my dad. Flipping heck.

'Kathy! Come out here now!'

As we walked back to our own block, myself crying pitifully, he barked I wasn't to go inside that flat again as everyone knew it was a 'drug den'! I said I hadn't had drugs, just beans on toast, but he was adamant that if I went there again he would kick my arse to kingdom come and back again and I believed him so I didn't.

I remember trying to find the beehive lady again but couldn't remember what block she lived in so one day I randomly knocked on one of the third-floor doors in a block from the outer row.

A very old man, peeking out from his chained door, answered.

'Does the lady with the poodle live here?' I asked.

'I don't like dogs,' he said.

'Me neither,' I replied, 'but she made me a bacon sandwich once and I'm hungry.'

'I don't eat bacon,' he said, 'I'm Jewish.'

'So's my mate Meir!' I happily exclaimed. 'He's from South Africa!'

He considered this, then after a beat said, 'I've got eggs.' So in I went.

It was sparse but clean with a whiff of disinfectant and in each corner of the front room were piles of newspapers. A framed wedding photo sat on the mantelpiece.

'Aah, is that your wedding?' I asked.

'Yes,' he replied, but gave no further information.

He had two boiled eggs but only gave me one – which I thought was a bit tight but said nothing except thank you. He peeled it for me then mashed it up in a bowl with salt and butter, which made me feel like a baby but, again, I said nothing. The bread was long and thin.

'What's that?' I asked.

'French stick,' he replied.

'Ooh la la!' I said, which made him smile. He tore off some bread, split it in half, scooped my mashed egg into it and added some sliced tomatoes. He squashed it together. His hands had newspaper print on them, which made the bread go dirty, but it didn't matter because it was absolutely delicious.

HUNGOVER I

Dad's hangovers were mighty. The large amounts of cheap alcohol he consumed over a couple of weeks' bingeing took its toll in the most gruesome of ways. Shakes, hallucinations, vomiting and the shits could go on for days. Our bedroom stank. If it was really bad I'd take my blankets into the living room to sleep on the sofa but he'd often cry out in the night that he needed company as he was 'dying'. 'Please, Kathy! Come back to the room! I'm dying here! I may not last the night!' So I'd reluctantly head back to my bed where he'd reach across from his own to hold my hand while he cried, farted and belched. He was good enough to keep the sick bucket on the other side of his bed.

John would be sent to the doctor to get a time-off note for work. Dad would spend the majority of this time in bed or on the loo. I would often be woken abruptly by his panicked night-mares or the pain from his tummy cramps. Dehydration was an issue. We kept old milk bottles, rinsed out and filled from the tap, ready in the fridge for these regular occasions. Lucozade was the other favourite. The boys or myself would be sent to the shop to buy a couple of bottles. I liked its bubbly glass and scrunchy orange wrapper.

When he was through the worst Dad would join us in the living room, taking his place in the chair by the fire, heart heavy in a gloom of remorse.

'That's it for me with the drink. I promise yous this is going to stop.'

And it would. For a while.

OTHER KIDS

I didn't really have any pals in the flats until I was a bit older. I think the kids thought I was weird. I can't say I blame them. On the outside of our ground-floor flat was a large tombstone-shaped plaque saying when the flats were built etc., but for some strange reason when I was little I told the other kids it was actually a gravestone and my mum was buried in it. Hence their avoidance evermore.

Nobody from school came to our house. I went to theirs. I liked going to Diane's the best. She lived near Dalston and her flats were modern with long walkways that looked out on to the street. There were lovely flower pots outside her front door. Her mum always had crisps in the cupboard, which I was allowed to help myself to. Crunch.

Once, Di and I found a discarded child's buggy and so began her favourite thing to do with me. I had no eyebrows and she loved to scoop my hair up tight into a bobble hat so I looked bald. She'd put a doll's dummy in my mouth, a teddy in my arms and with a blanket tucked tightly around my legs she'd wheel me up and down the Balls Pond Road, telling everyone I was her baby. We would cry with laughter at people's reactions and even more so at their indifference.

I would often see a cool-looking brother and sister who were a few years older than me walking around near my flats. One day when I was by myself in the swing park they asked if I'd like to play with them. I couldn't believe it. I was beside myself with excitement but acted cool, shrugged and said 'If you like.' They took me over to the umbrella. It was still huge to me. It had a wooden seat all the way round and the next tier up was metal, which you could hold on to or stand on if you were bigger.

'Lie down,' instructed the sister. The wooden seat was quite high from the ground and the umbrella itself was very wobbly.

'I'll fall off,' I said.

'No you won't,' she said, then told her brother to keep the umbrella steady. I stupidly lay down and the next thing I knew she was wrapping a large piece of rope around me and the seat, tying me to it. I began to panic.

'Don't do that!' I pleaded. 'I don't like it!'

But neither of them cared. They started laughing at my distress and, once they thought I was fully tied, started to spin the umbrella, running along with it as fast as they could. I felt sick with fear. The rope wasn't tight enough and I started to slip. 'Help!' I screamed. 'I'm going to fall off!' But this made them laugh even more. The next thing I knew I was in the air then on the hard ground a couple of feet away from the still-spinning contraption. My face grazed and stinging, through fat tears I watched them run off, still laughing. What a couple of cunts.

I spotted them again a few weeks later when I was out with Barry doing shopping chores. 'Those two nearly killed me in the park!' I shouted while pointing. Barry asked what had happened and I told him all the gory details. He put down the shopping bags, said 'Stay here' then went over and gave the boy a big slap round the chops, grabbed the girl as she tried to run off and shook her so hard I thought her brain was going to fall out. What a hero.

I got picked on a fair bit. The usual poking, pulling and

punching. I never wanted to hit back, especially if I liked the kid. Diane would push me around a bit but I only ever hit her back once. Hard. She stopped after that and we've remained great friends to this day.

DRY I

It was strange when Dad was sober. He'd go from a world of confusion to a man who didn't like his routine being upset. He'd wake at six, wash, shave and head out to work. In the winter months we'd hear the key in the door by five, summer, five-thirty. He'd eat his tea and watch TV with us, laughing his head off at *Dad's Army*. The rent would be paid and money for the weekly shop would be on the table.

He was stricter than usual and would give out the orders. If he was angry with me so I needed a clump, his aim was annoyingly better without the blur of the booze.

I liked sitting on his lap, happy with the irregular aroma of tobacco and soap.

He'd sometimes work on a Saturday morning but be home in time for the afternoon sport and a check on the football pools. Once in a while he'd cook. Boiled bacon, spuds and cabbage, all done in the same pot. He'd have a mug of the cooking liquid on the side along with a couple of slices of thickly buttered bread.

We'd go to Chapel Market on a Sunday morning to buy second-hand clothes and sausages in bulk. Sometimes we'd call on a friend of his who owned a newsagent's on Barnsbury Road. He'd give me some sweets and a small pack of tobacco for Dad. I liked getting it out of its tight little wrapper and decanting it into a pouch when we got home.

If the weather was good he'd take me to a park. Highbury Fields with its band-less bandstand or Clissold on Green Lanes. The latter was my favourite, it had small animals and a paddling pond. He'd chat away to other grown-ups. Women would be impressed with his dedication to me when he told them he was a widower.

'Aah, isn't he a good daddy taking you to the park? I hope you'll look after him when he's older.'

I'd smile and say of course I will, but inside I'd be thinking, *Fuck that.*

This time of peace could last a few weeks or even a couple of months but the absence of the sound of the key in the door at five, five-thirty was the indicator it was coming to an end.

He'd return around seven, tipsy, on the defence that he needed a couple of drinks without any of us saying anything. We knew the disease had regained its grip and the next evening he wouldn't return at all.

THE TOP-FLOOR FLAT

We were moved to the top-floor flat at the other end of Halton Mansions when I was around nine or ten, and I finally had a room of my own, as Virginia Woolf suggested we should. I could still hear Dad's excruciatingly loud snoring through the wall, but to finally have my own space was bliss. The other differences were a modern electric fire in the front room, so no more fetching heavy bags of coal from the yard, and how bright this room was compared to the ground-floor flat. We were again at the very end of the row, but the front room had an extra window at the side instead of a gravestone and we were above the trees. The council had newly decorated it for our arrival and Dad had purchased a brand-new three-piece suite. Everything felt fresh and clean. The brothers still had to share a bedroom but it was a bit bigger than their last one, which was handy as they were bigger too. My bedroom was tiny, more like a box room. It had a built-in wardrobe and just enough space for a small dressing table and single bed. I promised myself I would keep it spotless and everything would be in its proper place always, but this didn't last very long.

We were still in the middle row of blocks so the front looked over the green areas, and the back overlooked the bins and washing lines, but it felt so different. I had a proper view of all the comings and goings, which I loved as it made me feel quite superior.

The boys' room was next to the front room so four windows faced out front. There was quite a wide bit of guttering, more like a ledge that ran along just below the window frames. The council sent a cleaner to wash the windows as we were so high up, and he stood on the guttering, walking along. I remember sitting on the sofa, watching in awe, thinking to myself, *I'm going to try that next time the flat is empty.*

So I did. What a nutcase. I'm quite scared of heights now but obviously wasn't as a fearless kid. The first time I went out on to the ledge I kept my body close to the window, edging my way tentatively to the next one along. I soon got braver, though, and started to easily walk back and forth. There was a small square plinth attached to the wall and I would sit on it with a cuppa, catching a few rays. One time Barry was in his bedroom, sitting on the floor with his legs crossed, listening to a record through the headphones. At that time it was probably some Led Zeppelin or maybe the *Clockwork Orange* soundtrack album. I stood watching him for a while, enjoying my status as an unseen spy, but eventually I couldn't resist the urge to *knock, knock, knock!* He didn't so much jump out of his skin rather he bounced off the ground with his legs still crossed like a Ukrainian Cossack dancer or a levitating Aladdin.

'What the bloody hell are you doing?!'

I ran and dived back into the front room as he entered the proper way through the door.

'You silly little cow! I could've had a heart attack! What the hell were you doing out there?!'

I started crying. 'Nufink! Please don't tell Dad!' Which he wouldn't have done as we never grassed each other up to the pater. However, someone else in the flats must have because when Dad got wind of the situation, he quite rightly went bananas. 'You're nothing but a fecking eejit! You're a mad woman! You could've got yourself killed! Don't you ever fecking go out there again!'

So I didn't.

Nobby the cat would venture out there too but his balance must've been damaged from his wild fighting days as he fell off a couple of times, leading to him being fucked in the head, so we inevitably had to have him put to sleep. I remember crying on the morning he was taken to the vet but John told me recently we *all* cried including Dad. A therapist would have a field day about that now.

Our neighbours opposite were an older English couple called Hilda and Arthur. He had a room dedicated to his model railway, which I was allowed to look at but never touch, and she would make me cheese and piccalilli sandwiches. They had a grown-up daughter called Linda, and I used to spy through our double-lock keyhole at her and her boyfriend snogging on their doorstep on Friday nights.

The worst thing about living in the top-floor flat was carrying the shopping or laundry up the four flights of stairs. Even heavier than those was the bike Pat and Meir had bought me. It was a ladies' bike not a child's and it weighed a fucking ton. I could've chained it up downstairs but was worried about it getting nicked, it was too precious. After cycling around Islington for hours I'd pick it up and hoick it up the stairs, stopping on each floor to catch my breath or have a smoke before finally getting it safely to its home outside our new front door.

THE WORST THING I EVER DID?

I was in that weird pre-teen stage. Feeling like a 7-year-old and looking close to forty.

I hung around with a lovely girl called Jane for a while. She had a young mum and dad and an Old English sheepdog, which was the coolest thing in the world at the time, as its breed was used for a paint advert so was known in the flats as the 'Dulux dog'. I was scared of dogs but liked him or her from a distance. Another girl called Linda had my undivided for a bit but she was quite tough and liked to beat people up, myself included, so that friendship was pretty short-lived.

For a while I just seemed to wander around Upper Street, Essex Road and the blocks of flats off and in between. If I saw a group of kids up to something I'd join in. Hanging around in a small closed-down factory on Moon Street was a favourite. Brothers Chris and Tony would let me join them in smashing up stuff that was already smashed. We'd take little breaks to puff on fags nicked from their mum.

I once came across a boy sitting in an abandoned rust bucket of a car. His name was Lee, which made me think of America, and he let me sit in the back. He didn't have much to say for himself so I did all the talking. He was there again the next day and this time let me sit up front with him as I'd bought us both some sherbet Dip Dabs. I said, 'You can kiss me if you like?' Which was very brave of me as I'd never kissed a boy before.

But he said, 'Not today, maybe tomorrow.'

I got very excited that night, thinking about the possibilities of having a boyfriend, and dreamed about a boy I liked in primary school suddenly having a moustache. But the next day both the car and my pretend American boy were gone.

Liverpool Road runs parallel to Upper Street. There wasn't much to it except flats and massive houses. I was having a wander when a group of four lads around my age asked where I was going. 'Nowhere,' I said.

Then one of them said, 'We know this woman who lets us sit in her flat if it's cold. D'you wanna come?'

'Won't she mind?' I asked.

'Nah, she's got no kids and she's lonely. She lets us smoke.'

So with them I went.

Liz was Scottish and probably in her thirties. Her flat was nice and neat with lots of books on the shelves and potted plants on every surface. She gave me a cup of tea, herself a glass of wine and the boys a can of lager to share between them. And we smoked. She liked me. She thought I was funny especially when I did impressions of my dad and Billy Connolly and she was impressed at the difference between my Irish and Scottish accents, 'There's not many who know how to do that, hen.'

I went back the following week. The boys were already there, giggling away at something. Liz made tea for me in her small kitchen. 'They're laughing at my dirty book.' *The Happy Hooker* by Xaviera Hollander was a memoir about the author's life as a call girl in the '60s and early '70s. We joined the boys in the front room, I took the book from them and started to read. Out loud. It was filthy. I read Xaviera as a sultry, posh, English lady even though she was Dutch and invented different voices for the other characters involved in her hilarious and very dirty anecdotes. My audience thought it was brilliant. They were crying with laughter at my nonchalant way of relaying the words suck, cum and penis.

This continued for a few visits. We'd gather, Liz would give us drinks and fags, then we'd all get comfy and I'd read out a couple of chapters. Big laughs, especially from glassy-eyed Liz. Then one time, when we were on our own in the kitchen, she told me she was going to visit pals the following weekend so wouldn't be home but if she gave me a key could I water the plants for her? Oh yes, I enthused, of course I would.

'But,' she said, 'you're not to let those boys or anyone else in. D'you understand?'

Of course, I said, nodding away with happiness that she trusted me and not them.

She gave me the key and winked. 'Secret squirrel.'

When I let myself in the following weekend everything was in order. Liz had done a proper tidy and the little flat was sparkling. I made myself a cup of tea and proceeded to water her millions of plants. *Not too much, hen, don't drown them, just a wee thirst quencher.* I was nearly finished when I heard the metal letter box rattle. I froze. Then again: *rattle, rattle, rattle.* Liz told the boys she wasn't going to be home, so why the fuck were they here?

'Kaf! Open the door, mate, Liz said we could come!'

I knew this was a lie but I was shitting myself at the unexpected added responsibility. I went to the door. 'She told me not to let you in. Sorry! Come back next week.'

I heard whispered chatter then, 'Open the door, mate, we won't be long, Liz won't mind, she likes us not just you!'

My guilt at being her favourite made me feel hot so I opened the bloody door. In they stomped, pushing me to the side. It was only two of the usual boys and three bigger ones who I'd never seen in my life before.

'Who are these?' I squeaked at the regulars.

'My cousins,' came the reply. They went to the fridge and took out all the lager and all of the wine.

'You can't have that!' I implored. 'That's Liz's!'

'Piss off, you ugly bitch!'

Oh! I didn't expect that, I thought they loved me! I watched in despair as they guzzled the booze and started going through the kitchen drawers, tipping their contents on to the floor. I felt weak with sickness and started to cry. One of the 'cousins' snarled in my face, 'We told you to piss off!'

'But I'm in charge,' I answered pathetically.

'Wrong!' he said, '*I'm* in fucking charge!'

I was shaking now and thought I was going to wet myself, so I left and ran all the way home.

I should've gone back the next day to clear up the mess and wait for Liz to explain but I didn't. Instead, I stuck my head into a deep hole of denial. Maybe everything is okay? Maybe the boys tidied up and bought booze replacements? Maybe I dreamed it? By that Sunday evening I'd convinced myself that no real harm was done. I watched a bit of telly, got my bag ready for school and went to bed.

Bang! Bang! Bang! The knock at our door was horrific. It was nearly midnight. Unfortunately Dad was going through a dry spell so was there to answer. I was frozen in my bed. I heard deep voices and a high-pitched ramble that I recognised as Liz. *Oh shit, oh shit, oh shit!*

'Kathy!!! Get out here now!!!'

The police were there with a red-faced Liz. *The police!* The brothers had *never* brought the police to our door, even though Dad had many times. The shame! After much shouting back and forth between my dad and Liz, and embarrassed tears and stuttered explanations from me, Liz said she never wanted to see me again. I didn't want to see her again either, the old piss-head, but I didn't say that of course. The police told Dad he'd get a letter from the court if charges were pressed, and off they all went. I'd never seen our dad more angry during sobriety. Needless to say, he battered me then I crawled back into bed sobbing until I slept.

We heard nothing more about it.

EUSTON, WE HAVE A PROBLEM

My secondary school, Maria Fidelis School for girls, was in two buildings behind Euston Road, about a two-mile journey from home. I didn't like it. Not the school's fault, to be fair. Two separate schools had recently merged to make one big comprehensive, so a lot of the teachers had come from a top grammar school, used to teaching students with academic minds. I certainly wasn't one of those. I found most subjects boring, although I did excel at history for a couple of terms.

I made some great friends: Bernice had come with me from primary, Samantha was new, and Cathy and Mary became my closest. Mary and I used to go to and from school together as she lived off Upper Street. Cathy lived in Camden and I'd sometimes spend the weekend with her good-humoured family.

School was a nightmare of rules and regulations, incomprehensible lessons and millions of annoying, screeching girls everywhere I turned. Myself being the most annoying and screeching of them all.

I was constantly in trouble. I was fidgety, scratchy and too interested in being a funny twat, so I was infuriatingly disruptive. No teacher knew what to do with me. Except two: the librarian who wasn't really a teacher but would let me in the library anytime as she knew it kept me still; and an angel that was Sister Catherine, our home economics teacher.

She never asked questions. She would just see me in the corridor, know something was awry and say, 'Why don't you come into the kitchen with me for a bit of quiet time?' So I would. And it was lovely. Just me and her, making an apple crumble and talking about nothing.

I hated puberty. It felt weird and awkward. I knew about periods. The Galvin girls had filled me in on that front, but I was drifting away from them and the Corcorans. I no longer wanted to spend my Sundays with them. Instead, since we'd moved to the top-floor flat, I only wanted to be with my new best friend, Paula, who lived in the flat underneath with her English–Indian family.

She was a beauty. Like drop-dead, head-turning beauty from around twelve years old but carried herself with the maturity of someone in their late teens. Dangerous. I thought she was magnificent. She lived with her Indian nan who dressed in a Western way and smoked menthol cigarettes in an armchair all day long, her incredibly glamorous mum, Jean, who listened to Barry White and was brilliant at mimicking characters from the telly, her brother Joe who lived in his room and was obsessed with cricket, and her English dad whose name I can't remember but I do remember him being very nice.

I spent more time in Paula's flat than my own. It was clean and feminine and Paula's mum helped me out when my period started by giving me some pads and telling me what to expect.

School was even more of a slog during those times, though. I was constantly falling asleep and then being shouted at for it.

Many years later, when I was in my mid-forties, it was discovered that I was born with a blood condition called antiphospholipid syndrome, or Hughes syndrome to give its layman's name, and one of its many symptoms can be extreme tiredness. Go figure.

I bunked out of school a lot, of course. It seemed sensible at the time. Our school uniform was very distinctive with its blue blazer and kilt but I had an old letter from Dad regarding a doctor's appointment that I carried with me in case anyone asked why I wasn't in school. Nobody did. Wandering the streets wasn't the best fun especially if the weather was bitter, and it was colder for longer back then, but if Dad was on a binge it was easy to stay at home. Daytime telly didn't provide much except programmes for toddlers and middle-aged women but we had plenty of vinyl by then so I'd play records, use knitting needles for drumsticks and bash away badly on piles of whatever.

For a while I would go to this lovely boy Alan's house in Archway whose mum didn't mind him staying at home. I think he had some medical issues as he was quite small for his age and had a slightly wonky eye. I can't remember how I knew about him but I do remember boldly knocking on his door, introducing myself and asking if I could come in. Not a problem. He had a friend called Nige, who was always there, and a big fat orange cat. This was a great arrangement until his mum got wind of the situation because there was suddenly more food missing when she got home from work. I loved toast and they had a toaster whereas we still used the cooker grill at home. On the morning Alan told me he was sorry but his mum said he couldn't let me in any more I was very bereft. I loved hanging out with him, Nige and the cat. We played darts and cards and laughed so much. Oh well.

I never saw him again until one day in the early noughties when I was heading home in a black cab. The driver asked if I was Kathy and I said yes. He then went on to say, 'A mate of mine said we used to know you years ago but I honestly can't remember ever knowing you.' Oh, I said, where would that be etc.? He said his name and where he used to live and suddenly it came to me.

'Was your friend called Nige?'

Affirmative.

'Did you have a fat orange cat?'

Now startled, he confirmed this too.

But he didn't look like the Alan I was remembering until I asked, 'Didn't you used to have a wonky eye?'

He looked at me via the rear-view mirror, lifted up his glasses and said, 'Still do!'

And there it was in all its bright blue wonky beauty.

ATTENTION MUST BE PAID!

After my debut as the blackbird who pecked off the maid's nose, it felt like my acting days were over. Although my reading skills were put to use, nothing more came my way. I realised that I would have to create my own work. In my last year of primary school, I gathered some pals together who were willing to indulge me in an idea.

'Let's do a play,' I said. I knew about 'plays' from the telly, having never been to the theatre apart from that one pantomime trip. My story was about a family who were always arguing and I called it *The Happy Family*. After a couple of 'rehearsals', which was just me telling the others what they should do/say, we did our first performance in front of about three kids during a lunchtime. I loved it. It gave me a buzz so I encouraged the others to do it again the following day and the day after that. It probably only lasted five minutes and wasn't cutting into my cast's eating and skipping time too much, so they went along with it, even though they weren't as enthusiastic as me. And why would they be? Not only was I the writer and director but I was also the star. I played the mum of the family while the others were naughty siblings. They would have an argument and I would step in, do my best impression of an over-burdened adult, ask what the bloody hell was going on, then give a monologue on how we all needed to be happy. Our audience grew and by the last show we had a large circle around us, including some teachers. My 'mum' got big laughs, which I liked the best. It soon dwindled when everyone, including myself, got bored.

Outside of school the Corcorans' youngest daughter, Angela, would also do shows with me. We'd think of a story and I would inevitably play the leading role. I can't remember anything about the actual plays but I do recall Angela being a very good actor and Nellie and Denny indulging us with an audience whenever we'd shout, 'Ready!'

Drama wasn't on my secondary school's curriculum so once again I had to come up with something on my own. There was some charity thing going on in my first year there so I thought it would be good to do a couple of lunchtime shows – purely for charity purposes, of course, not so I could show off. The only thing I remember it involving was myself as the star, naturally, and my role being a cleaning lady who worked for the BBC – the British Bog Company. Big laughs again. No doubt this idea was probably nicked from *The Two Ronnies*.

By the time I got to third year, year nine in new money, I had forgotten my fancy ideas of becoming an actor as I'd got into music in a big way so thought music journalism could be a more realistic option. However, out of the blue, an English teacher, Mr Paul, replanted the acting seed.

He'd started to do some drama with us. Little improvised scenes that came from a book of ideas by someone called Anna Scher. I ended up doing my usual charladies or older women who were a bit sex-obsessed, my influences being Irene Handl and Dick Emery. After one particular lesson in which I got lots of laughs and cheers from my classmates, Mr Paul asked if I'd heard of the Anna Scher Theatre, which was based in Islington. I hadn't. I knew that kids from Islington were sometimes on the telly, Pauline Quirke and Linda Robson were already established TV stars, but I had no clue how they'd got there. Then a girl who I'd previously paid no attention to put up her hand, said she went there, sir, and all you had to do was put your name on a very long waiting list, so she'd put my name on it next time she was in. And that was that.

I spotted said girl in a corridor the following week and asked if my name was on the list. 'Oh, yes,' she said, 'but like I said, it's a very long list so you won't get in for a while.'

'How long?' I asked, thinking it could be a couple of months. 'I dunno,' she replied, 'about three years.' Then sauntered off.

Three years?! Flipping heck. That was a lifetime away for 13-year-old me. I would've left school by then and probably be a top journalist on the *NME* and living in my own flat overlooking Highbury Fields.

I'm very grateful for Mr Paul's encouragement because when I got to my last year of secondary I had to ask my form teacher to sign an application for further education college. Miss J, who scooped out cottage cheese from a small pot with cucumber sticks for her lunch every bleeding day, wasn't as positive.

'Can you sign my form please, miss?'

'What for?' she asked.

'Further education college.'

Her eyes widened. 'You?! To do what?'

'Drama, miss.'

'Drama?! And what do you intend to do with that?'

'I want to be an actress, miss.'

I think I gave her the biggest laugh of her career.

TEENAGE KICKS

Fuck me, I hated puberty. I didn't like my physical development and fashion wasn't doing it for me. Tight Levi jeans and boob tube tops didn't suit my manky teeth and rat's tail hair. I was a tomboy and liked shopkeepers calling me 'son' by mistake. I didn't want to *be* a boy, but I didn't want to be a girlie girl either. What to do?

Well, luckily for me it was 1977 and my saviour arrived kicking, spitting and screaming: punk rock! This was perfect. I was only thirteen so couldn't embrace it to the full but did my best with the little resources I had.

I went to a barbershop and had my straggly locks cropped close to the bone. School was not impressed, and of course neither was Dad, but I loved it. I then customised any clothing I owned by ripping, tearing and drawing on it. Someone at school showed me how to cut off the sharp bit of safety pins so they could be hooked into the mouth without piercing. Beautiful!

I started to buy the *NME* and *Melody Maker*. I couldn't go to gigs yet but I liked reading about them and cutting out pictures of bands for my bedroom wall. Most of my money now went on records. Paul Weller and The Jam were early favourites along with Blondie, The Clash, X-Ray Spex and Buzzcocks. John was now at art school so got to see a lot of the bands do their first gigs, which made me extremely jealous.

The famous Hope and Anchor pub on Upper Street was *the* place for up-and-coming bands, though. I was too young to actually go in, but I wandered up and down outside to see if I could spot any cool cats – and one day I did. The coolest of them all at the time: Johnny Rotten. I couldn't believe my eyes. Was it really him? I walked past and took a peek at the person chatting to a small crowd. It *was* him. Flipping heck! I turned around to walk past again, casually looking everywhere except in his direction. When I dared to glance over he caught my eye and was probably amused at my makeshift punk attire.

'Hello, little girl,' he said.

A million thoughts whizzed through my head. *What to say? What to say? What to say?!*

'Fuck off, Johnny!' came my reply, which earned big laughs from himself and the crowd. I carried on walking as if it was an everyday occurrence, but inside I was buzzing, delighted with myself.

Home life had changed as Islington Council were giving Halton Mansions a massive, much-needed facelift, so we were moved to a big house off the Essex Road. It had a nice-sized front room and John had some prints of artworks by Degas and Van Gogh framed. When Auntie Joan Galvin came to visit she commented, 'Blimey, that's the first time I've seen pictures on your walls.' Its large kitchen led into a garden with a pear tree but no partridge. The fruit was often rotten but salvageable ones were made into a pie by John. My bedroom was at the top next to Dad's room and the bathroom. The boys finally each had a bedroom of their own. They were both at college now, John doing the aforementioned art, Barry – economics. We only really saw each other at mealtimes or when there was something we all wanted to watch on the telly. Dad was still in his drunk-hungover-dry routine but the dry spells seemed to be getting longer – although the three of us had learned this was never to be fully trusted.

Paula and her family were moved into a newly built council estate in Archway. It was so modern, much nicer I thought than our house, which was big but cold. I would head to Paula's as much as possible, staying the night some Fridays and most Saturdays. We were so different. She was very much a girlie and didn't like punk, but we still had a laugh together.

She loved boys and the boys *loved* Paula. The second weekend I visited she suggested we go and hang out in a playground area on the estate.

'I saw some boys there in the week,' she said, 'one was *really* good-looking with blond hair cut into a wedge!'

So we went. We sat for a bit, me smoking, her smoking hot, and were eventually joined by a small gang of lads. We exchanged names and where everyone had been moved from. Of course all of them were much more interested in Paula than me. Except one. He didn't look particularly punky but he sat next to me then loudly sang some lyrics by The Clash into my face, so I loudly sang the next lines back into his.

His eyes nearly popped out of his head. 'You like The Clash?! I don't know any girls who like The Clash!'

'I *love* The Clash,' I replied. And, simple as that, I now had my first boyfriend. Of sorts.

Steve was a couple of years older than me and such a lovely boy. Really kind and very funny. He lived on the estate with his mum, dad and sister Julie who was pretty and sweet. Within a few weeks of knowing him he'd gone full punk. His hair was dyed black and soaped into spikes and he'd gained the punk uniform of skintight jeans and studded black leather jacket, just like Sid Vicious from the Sex Pistols. I thought he was amazing.

The main problem with him being older was I couldn't go to gigs or anywhere with him really. I'd only see him on weekends and even then for a short time before he headed out to pogo with proper punks, not silly little part-timers like me. I'd sit in his bedroom while he got ready, listening with envy about the gigs and parties he'd been to or was going to. Every now and then his angry dad would burst in and shout his head off at him. It never bothered me, I just thought most dads were mad, but it would upset and embarrass Steve, 'He's always having a go at me about something.' He'd bounce back pretty quickly, though. 'Oh well, he's just old I suppose, can't be much fun, eh?' Such a lovely boy.

I couldn't really be a proper girlfriend to him and I was too young for hanky-panky, which he never pushed for once I'd said, 'Best not, I don't want to end up preggers.' So, after a couple of months of lovely smooches and cuddles, we decided to amicably part ways.

He would come back into my life a couple of years later in an unexpected and dramatic way, but we'll leave him in this happier place for now.

As 1977 moved into '78, '79 and '80 an abundance of new bands and sounds had emerged. New wave and ska were making a big impact, particularly the latter with the genius 2 Tone Records. The release of the film *Quadrophenia* brought on the mod revival and every man, woman, child, dog, budgie and goldfish was in love with Debbie Harry. This period of time is all a bit of a mash-up for me as I chopped and changed from a punk to a skinhead to a mod to a skinhead again. I wanted to be in *all* the gangs. As I grew older and got more daring, girls at school who were into the same scene as me would let me know if a party or gig in someone's garage or back garden was happening at the weekend. I'd tell Dad the old chestnut that I was staying at someone's house, usually a fictional friend called Tracy, then head off into the night to unknown territories such as Ladbroke Grove or Shepherd's Bush.

Once I was at an all-night party in a squat somewhere miles away from home. I didn't know a soul – or where the hell I was. I'd heard there would be a meeting point in a pub on Carnaby Street but whoever I was going with didn't turn up so I took my chances on my own. Some boy told me to get on the back of his scooter and off we went. I was worried about my mascara running from my streaming eyes caused by the whizzing through the streets.

The party was great. Fantastic music and lots of free booze. I ended up snogging with a boy who'd been sniffing glue, and the taste of Evo-Stik lingered in my mouth for days after. In the early hours the noise of the party led to someone calling the police, which in itself led to mayhem. Everyone running this way and that. It was exhilarating, I felt like I was *in Quadrophenia*. But I was also absolutely shitting myself. I ended up running for ages with another girl until we were on a main road and reached a bus stop, where we decided to catch our breath and hopefully a bus. It must've been around four in the morning so nothing was coming. I threw up in the road and she gave me a chewing gum. We sat for an eternity until the sun and a bus heading to Piccadilly Circus finally turned up. I knew I could get to The Angel from there, so on we got. It was still stupidly early when

I got home. I snuck in as quietly as I could but was startled by John coming out of the loo, frowning when he saw me.

'Why are you back at this time?'

My answer was already prepared. 'Tracy and me had a big row last night so I got up early and left. She's a right cow. I'm going to bed. See ya later!'

NO PROBLEM WITH SAYING NO

If there was a positive to Dad's strictness it was me being too scared to do anything too bad. Sure, I lied about my whereabouts, bunked off school and was still nicking the odd bit of money from him when he was away with the drinkie fairies, but that was the extent of my badness. I smoked and was starting to drink the occasional can of booze but drugs were a definite no-no. Glue sniffing was a big thing for my generation, but I knew the eventual scabby mouth and nose would be a giveaway at home so I politely declined whenever a manky crisp bag full of the stuff was offered. Speed was the other favourite. The kids would move on to this once the over-the-counter Pro Plus was no longer working. I didn't fancy that either. I was twitchy and had the odd tic, so felt I needed slowing down not speeding up. But the main deterrent was fear of being caught. I couldn't imagine how bad the consequences would be if I brought the police to our door again, so I didn't.

I also had no problem with saying no to boys. Steve was a gentleman and respectful, but other boys not so much. I put up a fight a few times. The worst one I recall took place in a youth club in Camden. I went to a party with Cathy from school and was having a great time, acting the clown, trying to ingratiate myself with a new crowd. This included being very flirtatious with a very tall and very heavy-set boy whose name I can't remember. I gave it my best Carry On actress 'Ooh, you're handsome, I bet I'd feel warm with those big hands holding me.' He was one of those boys that no girl fancied because not only was he massive but he was also 'a bit odd in the head'. I didn't know this important detail until it was too late, I just enjoyed the laughs I was getting at his expense.

There was an unlit storeroom that people kept sneaking into for a kiss and a fumble and I took my turn with a boy called Daniel. He was a great kisser and I was getting well into the snogging and ended up lying down with him on a small pile of gym mats. The door kept opening and closing, which I paid no mind to. I just kept imagining that Daniel was my new boyfriend as I remained lost in his luscious lips. Suddenly he was gone. What? There was a scuffle, then a weight so heavy landing on me that I thought the roof had collapsed but it was the massive boy who was now on top of me, grinding his massive self into me and slobbering on my face. Help! I felt like I was suffocating. Get off! Help! Help! I pushed and poked at his face. Years of fighting with my brothers came into use as I got a grip of the hair on the back of his head and yank yank yanked with all my might. It did the trick.

'Ow! Fucking hell!' He rolled off, grabbing his head, and I bolted out of the room sharpish. The music was so loud in the main room I knew then nobody had heard me shouting. I looked around, searching for Cathy, when I spotted Daniel already snogging another girl on the dance floor. How charming.

The incident made me wary of boys. I wouldn't flirt any more in case it led them on, which I felt I had done with the massive odd boy. He didn't know me so how would he have known I was joking? I decided I wasn't going to take the risk and in future if I liked a boy I would let him do the flirting first.

It would be a long wait.

WORK IT

My teenage years were filled with work as I needed to pay for my records and music papers. Babysitting and the occasional job cleaning posh people's houses were already on the go, but I wanted something that was regular so I got a Saturday job at a bakery on Essex Road.

This was great fun. The manager, Anne, was a jolly Irish lady who was tiny but well packed and the other staff, whose names have long gone, were two older women who had worked there for years. We opened at 7.30 so I had to arrive by 7 a.m. to get everything laid out on the window shelves and front glass cabinet. My favourite, the hot counter, was filled with sausage rolls and steak and kidney pies. I'd always make sure to put a pie aside for my lunch as they were very popular. We got discounts and could take home any leftover bread or cakes as they'd be stale by Monday. Anne told me on the sly, 'Just put aside what you want in the morning.' So I did. Crusty loaves and apple turnovers were the requests from home.

The customers were mostly okay, we'd have a laugh with some of them, but now and again someone would chance it with me being young, saying I'd given them the wrong change or whatever so I'd call out to Anne. She'd enter from the back room, chest first, doing a sergeant major act then politely prove the customer wrong. If someone was really rude to me or just plain miserable I'd stick my nails into their produce as I was putting it into a bag.

My favourite regular was Doreen, who was blind. I was frightened of her at first, as I didn't know how to behave and would avoid serving her, but one time she came in later than usual and I was on my own. I braced myself. 'Hello Doreen, I'm Kathy the Saturday girl, you after your usual?'

She beamed at me, her lovely swimmy eyes focused on my eyebrow-less forehead. 'Yes please, love, small sliced white and a couple of jam tarts.'

There were three jam tarts left on the tray so I put all of them in a bag but only charged her for two along with the bread.

'See you next week,' she said as she was leaving.

Fuck knows why but I called after her, 'I think you'll *hear* me next week you mean!' She stopped for a moment, and so did my heart.

When she came back the following Saturday I was worried she might complain to Anne about me, but I fronted it out. 'Morning Doreen, do you want your usual?'

To my relief she smiled, 'Yes please, Kathy.'

I got the loaf and, again, snuck in an extra free jam tart and as she was leaving she called over her shoulder, 'Hear you next week, love!' Which made a couple of the customers laugh. Phew. I continued to give Doreen an extra tart every time she came in and neither of us said a word about it.

By the time I'd been working there for a year or so my confidence with the customers had grown. I would tell jokes to the regulars and slip the odd freebie to those I knew to be a bit poorer than most, having learned this from kind greengrocer Dave. I loved sitting in the back room at lunchtimes, eating a pie then having a cuppa, a smoke and a gossip with the ladies.

The area manager would show himself now and then. I knew he didn't like me, he told me to my face that I talked too much, but he left the job of sacking me to Anne. They didn't have proof that I'd been giving stuff away so the reason for my dismissal was 'being overfamiliar with the customers', which made me feel like a pervert.

I'd walk past a laundrette in the early evenings and became aware of a skinhead girl who would be inside, sitting on one of the machines.

Now that we'd moved to the big house I didn't really know anyone from this bit of Essex Road and was nervous about catching her eye, but I needn't have worried because when we did eventually clock each other she smiled and waved for me to come in. So I did.

Debbie was gorgeous. She had huge blue eyes with each individual eyelash painstakingly mascaraed.

'Do you like Madness?' she asked.

'Oh yea,' I said. 'And The Specials and The Selecter.'

'I'm so in love with Suggs,' she sighed, 'but he's got a girlfriend. I saw them outside the Hope and Anchor and she's really pretty.'

'You're really pretty too,' I said.

'Aw, thanks, mate. Yea, I do get asked out a lot. I waved you in cos I do service washes here after school. Fran the manager is really nice and is looking for someone to do Saturdays. D'you fancy it?'

And simple as that I had a new job and another new best friend.

I loved my job at the laundry. Fran was, indeed, really nice. She had short, fine hair that she managed to comb into the tiniest ponytail I'd ever seen and loads of kids and grandchildren who would pop in to say hello. Service washing was a doddle. I got fifty pence for each wash and sometimes a bit extra if the customer was generous with a tip. Some of the washes could be pretty stinky, particularly men's with their skid-marked pants full of holes, but Fran flagged up, 'Use rubber gloves for the bad ones and hold your breath!'

After a few months she asked for a quick chat in the back room. She made me a cuppa. 'You're a great little worker and the customers really like you . . .'

Flipping heck, I thought, *I'm getting the sack again.*

But she continued, 'You have to keep this top secret, come with me.' She then took me to a tight noisy corridor behind the line of washing machines and pointed to a button on the service-wash-only one. 'This starts the machine without the money needing to be put in. Don't do it with all your washes or the owner will get suspicious, but every now and then you can treat yourself to a bit extra.'

This was amazing. I was already making quite a bit of money, much more than at the bakery, and now I would have piles of fifty-pence pieces to spend on whatever I wanted.

'Thanks, Fran!'

THE OTHER WOMAN

John and Barry were starting to have girlfriends but never brought any of them home until Barry met *the one*. Carmelita Isabell-necessary-on-a-bike – to give her full name – turned up by Barry's side in 1980 and, with a couple of blips in the middle, didn't leave until her death in 2022. She fell into his arms at a party and he then apparently said, 'I'm never going to let you go.' She was gorgeous, diminutive and mighty. Her favourite word was 'perturbed'. She hailed from Hackney – her mixed heritage being Polish and Caribbean. She moved into Barry's bedroom after a couple of weeks, and two months after that they were married. Her mum and dad didn't approve so didn't attend the wedding at Hackney Town Hall or talk to her for about six months. She was heartbroken and madly in love all at the same time.

I was delighted to have another female in the house, especially one who was six years older and looked extremely cool with her part rockabilly part two-tone attire. I nearly messed the whole thing up on our very first meeting, though. *How can I make her like me?* I thought. *Oh, I know, I'll tell her a joke. A mildly racist joke. She'll like that.* But she didn't.

'What makes you think I would find that funny?' Her well-spoken voice had a slight East End hardness behind it.

I was mortified. 'Sorry,' I mumbled. 'Charlie Williams told it on the telly and he's coloured.'

'He's not *coloured*,' she said, 'and neither am I – and before you start using the rotten term, I'm not *half-caste* either!'

I was puzzled. 'What are you then?' I tentatively asked.

She gave me a mixed look of disdain and impatience. 'I'm a young *woman* called Carmelita who you can call *Carm* when and *if* I decide to like you.'

That was me well and truly told. I had to win her over, but eventually she came to like me. She would only cook for herself and Barry, which was a huge disappointment. I was hoping she'd take over the kitchen like a good little woman, but she made it very clear that wouldn't be happening. 'I'm married to *him*, not you lot.' She'd sometimes make Barry a meal called steak-à-la-Carm, where she'd concoct a creamy, peppery sauce to go with the meat. The smell would waft up the stairs, tempting me down into the kitchen to quickly mop up the leftover juices from the pan with a hunk of bread before Dad or John could get to it.

Dad thought Carm was fantastic and would proudly announce to everyone how Barry had 'got himself a nice little coloured girl'.

But if I was in earshot I'd roll my eyes, tut-tut-tut and say with an air of patronising authority, 'She's not *coloured*, Dad! She's not flipping red, gold and blue!'

My wonderful world of wokeness had arrived.

THE WRONG IMPRESSION

I loved my skinhead look. On Sunday mornings I'd head to Petticoat Lane Market in London's East End to rummage through second-hand clothing stalls for Ben Sherman and Fred Perry shirts. It was also a good time to chat with boys. I liked talking about music and films but as time went on these boys seemed to only want to talk about politics – and the wrong sort of politics, meaning right wing, meaning racist. The National Front and British Movement had been hijacking pubs and gigs involving bands that the skinhead kids were into, dropping leaflets for their meetings and selling their newspapers. I knew their politics were horrible and certainly not the way I or my family thought about things, but I found it hard to drag myself away from the culture, especially as I'd spent loads of my money on getting the right clothes.

Paula's lovely mum Jean was really unhappy with my look, which was totally understandable, especially with her being of Indian descent. I went round to theirs with my new friend Tania to try and reassure her that for me it was all about music and fashion. Jean wasn't convinced. This beautiful woman who had been so kind to me from the age of ten no longer trusted me. At the time I thought she was being ridiculous and over-reacting but, looking back, I can't blame her for feeling the way she did.

Tania, like all my best friends, was extremely pretty. She had the skinhead look in her attire but couldn't bring herself to cut off her long blonde locks. She was troubled and really fucking angry with the world. She liked to get into fights although she was never like that with me. We always had a laugh together, smoking and drinking her stepmum's Martini with lemonade.

She also got involved with a very scary boy called Chris. He would fight on the football terraces and she would join him. I'm so glad I was a cowardly custard back then, meaning I never took part in that particular madness.

Debbie from the laundry, her friend Jane (who was funny like myself) and I would go to gigs together. I would usually only get to see support acts as I had to be home before the main event. One time, though, the band Bad Manners were playing at the Electric Ballroom in Camden. I can't remember why I was there on my own but I was. It was a Sunday night and there wasn't any school the next day so must've been during a holiday time. The gig itself was great fun, and I loved jumping up and down in my own world, covered in sweat and thrown-about beer. Trying to leave the gig, though, was horrendous. The police had locked the doors and were only letting a few people out at a time, causing a bottleneck. I was caught right in the middle. I was still really small, having not yet reached my overbearing 5 foot 3 and was getting squeezed and lost in the throng. Then the crowd started chanting 'Skinheads, skinheads!' I was shitting myself and thought I was going to die. What a way to go.

After what felt like an eternity, my section of the bottleneck was let out of the doors and I ran and ran and ran. I remember sitting on my bed back at home, still shaking and thinking to myself *Maybe I'm the wrong type to be a skinhead?* I remember calling a Black girl in primary school a racial slur, but that was the extent of my racism as far as I could recall. Maybe I should go back to being a mod or a punk? But I had plans to go to

Mum and Dad's wedding day, October 1954

Barry, me and John, 1964

Wearing my favourite coat,
aged two or three

Me, aged three, with Micheal and
Siobhan Galvin

Me, aged around five, outside Pat Cook's flat
with her mum and dad, Mr and Mrs Cook

Me, aged around six, with
groovy Pat Cook

John, me (aged seven or eight),
Pat Cook and Barry in Pat's flat

Laughing in a photo booth,
aged fifteen, with Debbie's
head at the bottom

Me, aged sixteen, seriously thinking
my skinhead days should be over

Michael, my best friend from college,
in rehearsals for a gig

Scrubbers: my first professional
acting job, slopping out scene

Barry and Carm's wedding day, 1980

Chloe Webb, Gary Oldman, me and Sara Sugarman
on the boat for *Sid and Nancy*

Dad, me and John on my twenty-first birthday

Me and Joe Strummer in Almería during *Straight to Hell*

Beating René Assa at poker in the hotel bar,
Granada, Nicaragua

Making the film *Walker* in Nicaragua
and telling Alex Cox I wasn't happy

Alex tells me he'll sort things out

Tilly, Michèle, Elaine and me, pissed in the Old Red Lion

With Tony and Pauline, pissed again in the Old Red

A platonic smooch with Perry Fenwick

Bananarama and Lananeeneenoonoo
for Comic Relief

Rowland Rivron as Dr Scrote and
me as pregnant Tina Bishop for
The Last Resort

Lovely Simon Brint and me,
pissed (again!) in the Old Red

Southend on the next bank holiday and really didn't want to miss out.

Quadrophenia had depicted fights between mods and rockers in the seaside town of Brighton and the kids of my era had latched on. I didn't want to get into fights, I just wanted to find a boyfriend who liked music and read books, so off I went on my own. It was incredibly boring. I walked around for a bit, sat in a cafe, had a cheese sandwich and a cup of tea, didn't go anywhere near where the trouble was and got on a train home just after lunchtime where I fought off a boy with *green* teeth who was trying to kiss me.

What a waste of time and hard-earned money.

Flipping heck.

The next day when I went to the newsagent's the papers were full of 'the disgusting behaviour brought to our beautiful seaside resorts by thugs and hooligans'.

There were lots of photos of young people fighting, but one particular photo made the front page with the word 'SCUM' blazoned across the top. It showed a boy being arrested who was snarling aggressively straight down the camera lens with his two fingers up to the world and the words 'MADE IN LONDON' tattooed upon his shaven head. My jaw dropped to the floor. I couldn't believe what I was seeing. It was Steve, my lovely first boyfriend. Steve? What the fuck?!

I went straight to the phone box on the corner of our street and rang Steve's number, which I still knew off by heart. Engaged tone. I tried for a while and eventually it rang and his sister Julie picked up. She was crying. I hadn't seen either of them for ages, so I felt a bit weird and didn't really know what to say.

'Blimey, Julie, what happened to him?'

'He got in with a bad crowd,' she sniffed, 'one minute he was all punky, the next he looked like that! He's in the nick and he'll probably be sent down, but we won't know what'll happen for a while yet.'

Sometime later the outcome was indeed Steve having to spend time in a detention centre, but before then he had to go to a hospital to have a couple of tattoos removed from his neck. One said 'FUCK OFF' and the other was a swastika, which were considered offensive. Go figure. I was allowed to visit him.

He was in a normal ward but a policeman was outside to keep an eye on things. He looked very sheepish sat in bed wearing hospital pyjamas and bandages covering the wounds on his neck.

'Kaf!' He couldn't believe I was there.

'Alright, mate,' I said. 'Fancy seeing you here.'

He told me he was off his head on drugs and booze when he had the tattoos done, encouraged by the new crowd he'd got himself involved with and he deeply regretted upsetting his mum. 'I've brought shame on the family apparently.'

He was being sent to the detention centre for a few months. 'Can I have your address?' he asked. 'Then I can write to you.'

'Okay,' I said, 'but I can't be your girlfriend again cos my dad would kill me.'

'That's alright,' he said, 'I've got a girlfriend, she's popping in later.'

Oh.

We wrote a couple of letters to each other. One included him telling me he was enjoying working in the small farm section at the centre, especially as a sow he loved had given birth to some piglets. 'I was allowed to name them,' he wrote, 'and I've called one of them Kath.'

Oh. Again.

The hospital visit was the last time I saw him. I used to bump into his sister Julie and her boyfriend Peter shopping up The Angel. They would tell me Steve wasn't in a good place, an addiction had got hold. Then eventually, I think it might have been in the '90s, the inevitable sad news came that he had died.

Despite the story the infamous photo of Steve tells, I have always remembered him fondly as the very lovely boy he once was.

BETTER THAN CHRISTMAS

Nineteen eighty was a great year for me. Despite my form teacher's misgivings I'd got myself into Kingsway Further Education College to study drama, film studies and, er, motor car maintenance. (Fuck knows.) But before then, I still had to finish school, which was tedious. The exams were a waste of time, but at least they meant I didn't have to spend the whole day there and had lots of free time in between. One day a wonderful thing happened.

Back then you could do a straight walk through Euston and King's Cross stations across the platform areas and this would be the start of mine and Mary's walk home from school. Mary, a lovely petite blonde, was of Irish heritage and the eldest of three. She wasn't into the punk/skinhead scene like me but she always indulged my non-stop chattering about my favourite bands of the moment. We also loved talking about all the boyfriends we didn't yet have and what sort of life we wanted in the future. Mine was obviously fame and fortune, hers the more realistic ambition of finding a nice boy and having a family.

The latest edition of the *NME* was in my bag. Ian Curtis – who was lead singer and lyricist of the band Joy Division – had died and a haunting photograph of the band walking away from the camera and entering a gloomy subway was on the front cover.

We'd walked through Euston Station and the back streets of Euston Road until we reached King's Cross, jabbering all the while, when suddenly by the tracks my own tracks stopped. I'd spotted a punk who looked like Paul Simonon from The Clash. Hang on, it *was* Paul Simonon from The Clash. And, there was

Mick Jones and, flipping heck, Topper Headon *and* the coolest of them all, Joe flipping Strummer! I grabbed Mary's arm, 'Mare, Mare, I can't breathe, that's The Clash, Mare, The Clash!'

'Who?' she asked.

I pulled up the sleeve of my white school shirt to show her my forearm, where a few weeks previously I'd scratched 'CLASH' on to it with a compass needle. 'The Clash, Mare!'

'Blimey,' she replied.

We huddled for a moment, trying to work out what to do while keeping an eye on the band and their small entourage. Then I remembered the *NME* in my bag. Perfect. I approached Joe Strummer, with Mary following.

'Alright, Joe?'

To my relief he smiled. 'Hello, there. How you doing? We've just missed our train.'

I took the *NME* and a biro from my bag. 'Could you sign this for me, please? It might make it worth something.'

He laughed, 'I doubt that but sure, no problem.'

As he signed, Paul Simonon came over and asked, 'Shall I sign it too?'

My reply was very bawdy, '*You* can do what you like!' Which made them both laugh. Joe then called over Topper and Mick so I had the full set. I acted cool, telling them again that I only wanted their autographs to make the paper worth something, but my knees were wobbling and my insides were screaming. I chatted on, saying I was nearly finished at school and couldn't wait for it to end *blah blah blah*, when Joe spotted the scratched 'CLASH' on my arm.

'Oh yeah,' I said, 'a mate was supposed to be getting some Indian ink for it but she let me down.'

He shook his head, 'Nah, don't be doing that to yourself in our name, man! You'll destroy your beautiful skin.'

Beautiful skin? No one had ever told me my skin was beautiful. I was elated but just shrugged and said, 'Okay, Joe, I won't.' And I didn't.

One of the entourage was only a couple of years older than me. He hung back while the band said goodbye and sauntered off to WHSmith's. Maybe he could sense a kindred spirit because from nowhere he said, 'Things were bad for me at home so I started hanging around with the band and now I go on the road with them to do running around for them and stuff. They're doing London gigs in a few weeks. You should come and maybe you could get a job with them too if you're leaving school and that.'

Everything stopped.

Could I really do that? Could I really run away with the funky-punky circus? Things weren't too bad at home. The year before had been difficult. Dad, John and Barry had one of their many massive fights, ending with Barry knocking Dad to the floor with a punch. I was at school when I was called out of the classroom to go to the Head's office. My body went cold. I thought she was going to tell me Dad had died, but no; Barry was leaving home for a bit to stay with a friend till the dust had settled and, because John was now at college, I would be on my own most of the time with Dad (and his drinkie rages), so there was an option for me to go into a children's home. I certainly didn't want *that*. A girl I knew called Janet was in a children's home. I visited her once. On the surface it seemed fine. Lots of kids running around making noise, and her shared bedroom was large with posters on the walls.

'This feels like a great place,' I naively said.

'It isn't,' said Janet, 'me and my roommate have to barricade the door at night to stop the older boys barging in wanting sex *and* a couple of the carers are dodgy too. I bloody hate it here.'

So my decision to stay at home with Dad was easy. Anyway, I was used to his drinking and knew how to handle him, but other grown-ups being in charge of me would be a whole different ballgame and I wasn't prepared to start again. Plus, in the year since Barry's punch, Dad had sorted himself out enough to get a job as a park keeper with the council, which was so much better than the back-breaking toil on the building sites. He enjoyed it and for the first time in his life was happy at work, which in turn helped the boozing ease off.

If I ran away from home now, when things were finally looking better, it could really fuck things up for him *and* my brothers, who quite frankly didn't deserve any more grief. The thought of knocking around with The Clash and this kind boy who obviously liked me was the biggest temptation I'd had in my life so far, but something else quite wonderful had happened and I didn't want to fuck that up either.

Back at King's Cross I snapped out of my reverie.

'Aw, thanks, mate,' I said to the kind boy, 'it's really nice of you to tell me that, but the thing is I've been waiting ages to get into a place called the Anna Scher Theatre cos I want to do acting and that, and the letter came through on Monday that I've finally got in so I'm gonna start going next week.'

It truly was my fork-in-the-road moment, and I look back without a beat of regret at the path I chose to take.

PART TWO

PART TWO

LIFE CHANGERS

When Anna Scher and her husband and work partner Charles Verrall passed away within a month of each other in 2023, I was asked by the *Guardian* newspaper to write a short piece to add to Anna's obituary.

I decided to write about my first time going and this was it:

You're nearly 16 and finally there. You've been on the waiting list for three years.

Walking into the large black room, knees wobbling, you feel a tangible vibrancy of hundreds of kids that came before you and hundreds more still to come. It's charged.

Old battered chairs line the walls. You sit in one closest to the door. Nobody notice me, please. Nobody does. The 50 or so other kids are too busy with their chat, their excitement, their . . . what's that thing I don't recognise from normal school? Oh yes, their happiness.

The clatter of a football rattle cuts through the babble. She's here.

You recognise her from a documentary on the telly and articles in the Islington Gazette. Long, thick hair. Knee-high boots and the most amazing teeth you've ever seen.

It's so quiet! Her voice has a sweet Irish lilt. 'Hello everybody and welcome. Our inspiration for this term is Dr Martin Luther King and our word of the week is strength.' You notice 'strength' on a card on a wall. 'We can show strength in many different ways, but is it always a positive thing? I look forward to your interpretations and improvisations. Now, is anyone new this evening?'

Your bum squeaks. Six or so other kids put up their hands so you put up yours.

'Welcome all of you. We start each lesson with a warm-up. Feel free to join in or sit and watch.'

What's a warm-up? Soul Limbo by Booker T & The MG's blasts out from the speakers. Anna at the front, the kids lined in rows copying her every move. This way, that way, clap, smile, stomp. That way, this way, stomp, smile, clap. Then it stops and everyone sits.

For the next two hours you learn about 'being a good audience' and how 'listening is the key to good improvisation'. You watch the others work their way through situations set by Anna. Kids from different backgrounds pretending to be their parents, teachers, friends or foes. Putting themselves in other people's shoes. Understanding life from another's point of view.

And when someone is brilliant or hilarious or both, the exuberant roar of appreciation and manic stomping of feet from us, the good audience, is fucking exhilarating. You're exhausted. You've never felt like this before. You've never respected and loved a teacher like this before.

In the shortest amount of time, this magnificent woman has become your everything.

That first lesson was such an amazing and exhausting experience that when I got home, which was only around eight-thirty, I went straight to bed and slept through for what felt like the first time in my life till seven the next morning, and I hadn't done anything except listen.

It was a magical place. Kids of all ages and backgrounds mingled together, shouting improvised sketches with the constant sound of laughter ringing through the air.

Anna was strict, though, 'Are you chewing gum? Then get rid of it *now*, please!' And, 'If you're late to my class it shows a lack of respect to myself and everyone else so please leave and we'll see you next time, *on* time!'

My first few months there were continuous listening and watching. Some of the kids would moan that Anna never picked them to do stuff or she only picked her favourites, but I didn't have a problem with that. I was happy to sit back and learn and I'd gleaned everyone got a go at doing something eventually, you just had to be patient.

The first time I spoke in front of the class felt amazing. Anna had decided that she wanted to hear from 'all those who haven't stood up today, bring your chair to the front and sit in an orderly line, please.' There were about ten of us and I was bang in the middle. 'I want you to tell us your name and life story in under two minutes.' The kids before me did a bog-standard telling of who they were etc. but with no colour and certainly no laughs from our audience. I remember thinking *I need to be a bit more lively* as this was my first and possibly only chance to make an impression.

My heart was thumping and when my turn came I nonchalantly said, 'My name's Kathy Burke and I was born. What a happy day . . .' I couldn't continue as there was laughter so I smiled, waited, then, 'Dad, Pat, came over from Galway, Mum, Bridget from Cork . . .' This made Anna sit up, as I slyly knew it would, being from Cork herself. 'I've two older brothers, who enjoyed a happy life till eighteen months after I plonked out . . .'

more laughter . . . 'when my mum sadly died.' There was a gasp
and noises of sadness and pity . . . 'It's okay,' I said, reassuring
the crowd, 'I think I'm over it.' And there it was, my first round
of applause.

Anna asked for a quick chat at the end of the lesson. Was it
my dad who worked in the park across the road, who she spoke
with a while ago? He was wearing a red woollen hat?

Flipping heck. I remembered Dad saying, 'I popped into the
Anna Scher place to see where your name was on the list and
Anna herself was there and we had a great little chat about
Ireland. She's a lovely woman.' I was furious. Why was he inter-
fering?! He didn't interfere with John's art or Barry's football so
why the hell would he do that with me?

'I was only there for a moment! Jesus, Kathy, don't be giving
out to me!' And then the reason for my anger dawned on him.
'I hadn't been drinking. I was *working* and went over during my
break.'

Oh. I softened. 'What did she say then?'

'She checked the list and said it'll be a while yet but she
looked forward to you joining them.'

'Yeah,' I said to Anna, 'that's my dad but he's in a different
park now so won't be bothering you again.'

She laughed, not knowing I was serious, so I laughed too,
pretending it was a joke.

A couple of lessons later I was picked to do an improvisation.

Anna would give us an opening line to say to an imaginary
partner and this time it was, 'Where were you? I've been here
for ages.' We all stood up, she gave us the 'Off you go!' and a
cacophony of words and tones filled the room as nearly forty
kids shouted their heads off to a space in front of them on

the outrage of being kept waiting. The football rattle was spun and we all dropped to the floor in silence. A girl was picked, up she got, shout, shout, shout, end, ripple of applause. A boy was picked, up he got, shout, shout, shout, end, ripple of applause, with an added 'whoop!' from his friends. A few more did their bits and I was really enjoying it all, until the unexpected and shocking sound of my own name came out from Anna's mouth.

I stood up. I was terrified. I didn't like it. I felt like a big fat giant standing in a sea of upturned heads. I croaked out the opening line, 'Where were you? I've been here for ages.' The timidity in my voice sounded pathetic. I went to say my next improvised line but it got stuck in my throat so I gave it another go but again the words preferred to stay in my gullet. However, for some reason my eyes didn't waver but stayed focused on my imaginary foe, which must've given the impression that I was *pretending* to try to say something because a couple of the group started to snigger, so I gave a small pause then actually *acted* that I couldn't get the next line out and then added extra acting to make the audience believe that my imaginary character was the one doing all the talking and wouldn't let me get a word in. This time the sniggers turned into proper laughter, so for the next thirty seconds I didn't say anything, just reacted by rolling my eyes, took a quick glance to another direction as if the space was telling me *Over there!*, a slight shake of the head, then threw in a 'But', which got a bigger laugh, paused again then ended with, 'Sorry about that, mate, my mistake.' I sat down to the sound of massive laughs, cheers and feet stomping, which was so loud I thought my eardrums were going to burst.

Anna was beaming and stood up from her chair, '*That*, boys and girls, was a small masterclass in the art of *listening*. Well done, Kathy Burke!' Everyone clapped and cheered again, and that night I couldn't sleep at all.

FURTHER EDUCATION?

On my first day at Kingsway Further Education College I made two new best friends, the first of whom had no interest in the role. I'd taken the 73 bus down to King's Cross and as I was walking up Gray's Inn Road towards the college I spotted a boy across the road walking in the same direction. He was wearing the mod attire of jeans, Fred Perry shirt and Hush Puppies shoes and was very good-looking.

'Hello,' I said, falling in step beside him, 'are you going to Kingsway?'

He was a little startled but took a quick glance at me and said nothing more than 'Yes'.

'Are you doing drama?' I asked hopefully.

He was repulsed, 'Absolutely *not*, I'm doing music and art.'

'Ooh, that's cool,' I said, 'my brother John does art, he went to St Martin's.'

He gave an impressed flinch then a reluctant reply of 'Michael' when I asked for his name.

'I'm Kathy, I'll come and find you at lunchtime if that's cool?' Then I hurried ahead so he couldn't say it wasn't.

My first couple of days were filled with class enrolling, working my way around the building and, most importantly, sitting in the best spot of the canteen where I could keep an eye on all the other students coming and going, trying to spot Michael. A plate of chips and a cup of tea were 15p, which I paid for with luncheon vouchers, plus I got a grant of £1,000 for my two-year course so I felt super rich.

Ange approached me in the canteen on day two. An attractive

and trim mixed-heritage girl from Stepney Green, her first question to me was, 'Are you a racist?'

I was still a skinhead so her query wasn't unfounded. 'No, I'm not,' I confidently replied, 'my sister-in-law is mixed race so I can't be or my brother would batter me.' Ange was very happy with that.

'I'm in the same drama class as you,' she said, 'so we should hang out together.'

Oh. Okay.

The drama classes were good but not brilliant. Included in the curriculum was dance, which I felt very awkward about as we had to wear a leotard and leggings, but the teacher said I had good rhythm, which made me feel a wee bit better. I dropped out of motor car maintenance after two lessons, which was a good idea as to this day I've never owned a car, but I absolutely loved film studies and made sure I attended every lesson given by an American teacher called Jack.

I found Michael again by the end of the week. He was in the canteen with a boy called Spencer. 'There you are, mate! I thought you might've dropped out. How's it going?'

So poor Michael – who confessed a while later that he'd actually been avoiding me – was now officially my first boy *friend* once I'd reassured him that I had no romantic interest because I was far too busy with Anna Scher's, my Saturday job and now college. Mind you, he did have an incredibly beautiful mouth, so if he'd wanted me to be his girlfriend I think I would've said yes. After he'd got to know me properly he liked having me around, as he found me 'cute, funny and a bit mad'. Perfect.

Michael was lead singer of a band called The Variations, whose inspiration were The Beatles and The Jam/The Style Council.

This was amazing. I didn't know anyone in a band and now my new best mate was inviting me to their rehearsals, which I went to often. They were terrific and Michael a really gifted singer-songwriter.

The only problem was I heard a rumour some people were referring to me as a 'groupie'. *A groupie?!* What the fuck! I convinced Micky (as he now wanted to be called) the only way to dispel this rotten falsehood was if I were to become the group's manager. Now, I didn't exactly know what I was supposed to do as a manager of an up-and-coming band, but I had already sorted them a gig at Kingsway so felt I'd proved myself as a good candidate. I was put on a three-month trial and was sacked within two.

I liked knocking around with Micky in the small flat he shared with his mum, Gloria, in Shoreditch. The first time I went she cooked us all sausages, mashed potatoes and peas with a spectacular homemade gravy. The second time I hovered as she made sausages and chips.

'Have you had your tea yet?' she asked.

'No.'

So she made me a smaller plate up with one sausage and a few chips. But the third time I turned up she made it very clear, 'I can't keep giving you your dinner! I've only got enough in my budget for me and him so you'll just have to wait in his bedroom till we're finished.'

I sat on his bed, listening to records and having a smoke, when it suddenly dawned on me at the grand old age of sixteen: *Fucking hell, Kath, we're* all *poor!* I remembered the meals that had been shared with me over the years and I don't know why I assumed everyone had more money than us, but I did. Maybe it was because everyone had 'stuff' like ornaments and jewellery? Gloria had finally put me right on that score and I never took a meal at somebody's house again unless I'd been invited to beforehand.

Ange was daft as a brush. One day when we went to a shop near the college to get some smokes she declared to the bloke behind the counter, 'We're actresses!'

The guy was impressed, 'Really? What have you been in?'

Ange didn't flinch, 'We're making a film at the moment, it's not at the pictures till next year so keep an eye out.'

'I will!' said the man. 'What's it called?'

'Juicy Bodies,' replied Ange. 'Go with a mate, not your wife. See ya!'

I went to her house in Stepney a few times but not as often as she wanted because it was a faff to get to from Islington. I could walk home from Micky's but would stay the night at Ange's. She was madly in love with some boy and would talk about him for hours on end. One time she had a birthday party in the local community centre, I think mainly in the hope of getting the boy back, and asked if I'd work behind the bar as, 'You won't really know anyone so best you have something to do, eh?' I agreed but soon realised I would be giving my services for free as, 'That can be your present for me. Thanks, babe.' The only thing I remember of the party was a constant playing of 'Oops Upside Your Head' by The Gap Band and an overwhelming smell of Malibu and pineapple juice that stayed in my nose pipes for weeks.

The Variations started to do gigs at a pub called the Mildmay Tavern off Balls Pond Road, organised by their newly found, more managerial manager. I'd been to the famous Hope and

Anchor on Upper Street a few times with Mary, in fact she met her future husband, Bobby, on our second time going. It was great to finally be inside as opposed to wandering around outside like a twit, but they wouldn't serve us alcohol because we were underage, plus John and Barry occasionally drank there and I didn't really want to be in a place where my big brothers could keep an eye on me, so the Mildmay became my first regular pub. It was known as a 'mod pub' and could be quite exciting when loads of young people rode up on their Vespa or Lambretta scooters before a night of revelry, its landlady not caring about age. I had lots of nice kisses and a few not so nice ones. Skinheads were absolutely not welcome, but I'd started growing my hair by then and adapting my clothes, which pleased everyone including myself, Paula's lovely mum Jean and especially Carmelita: 'I have to say I felt very perturbed when I first saw you with that horrible haircut. You looked like a stupid little wanker.'

On a political front I was Labour through and through, like my family. Thatcher, who I hated with a passion, was at the helm and I couldn't wait to be eligible to vote as I was certain my generation would boot her out. They didn't. I was also becoming increasingly proud of my Irish heritage. I became more interested through learning about the misadventures the British Crown and government had bestowed upon Ireland and its people. I watched the news more and started to read the *Guardian*, which John or Barry would buy. College would organise political events such as raising money for disadvantaged students or rallies for nuclear disarmament. I had lots of CND badges.

I don't remember doing much work at Kingsway, to be honest, and my first exam for drama was rendered ungraded so there was the proof. It didn't look like I was going to be let back for the second year but Jack, my film studies tutor, persuaded the powers that be to give me another chance as I had proved myself quite studious in his classes.

I only went back for the first term, though, as something quite unexpected and extremely exciting had happened.

AN IMPOSSIBLE SITUATION

My first year or so at Anna Scher's was wonderful. I really loved Anna, her gorgeous partner Charles, the improvisations and made-up ten-minute plays. I'd also acquired yet another new best friend. Elaine Lordan was loud, funny and extremely pretty with huge brown eyes and the whitest teeth I'd ever seen. She lived in Highbury with her Irish parents, Bernie and Garrett, and big sister Sophia. She'd been attending Anna's since childhood and had already done some professional acting work, most notably in the West End musical *Annie*. She walked with me to the bus stop after one of Anna's sessions, told me she thought I was brilliant and wanted to be my friend. So she was.

I had resigned myself to the fact I probably wouldn't make it as an actor. The Equity union had strict guidelines back then and as I was now over sixteen I wouldn't be able to get a union card until I'd done forty weeks of professional work, but I couldn't do professional work without a card, which was an impossible catch-22 situation. I was sad that I would never get into Anna's coveted 'professional actors' group' that took place on Friday evenings, but was determined to still enjoy my time there. I was finally getting stuck into college work and seeing if there was a way I could do a journalism course, as my ambition to write for the *NME* was still floating around my head.

At Anna's, directors, producers, casting directors and the like would often sit at the back of the room, watching the classes for potential bookings. I no longer got excited about this because of my no Equity card situation, so just got on with having a great time ripping off Irene Handl, until one day when Anna asked to talk to me after the class.

A director called Mai Zetterling had been in as she was casting for a film called *Scrubbers*, which was going to be the female equivalent of the brilliant Alan Clarke film set in a boys' borstal called *Scum*, and she wanted me to go in for an audition. *Me? Was Anna sure about that? But I didn't have an Equity card?* Anna said, yes that could be a problem but not to worry about it for now and just make sure I was ten minutes early as punctuality was *imperative*.

Everyone was home when I shared the news. John, Barry and Carm were excited for me, but Dad was a little quiet. He was worried, 'I've heard terrible things about that industry, casting couches and the like . . .'

I guffawed! 'Don't be fucking daft! That ain't gonna happen to *me*, they're after all the pretty girls. Anyway, the director's a lady who used to be an actress. Mai Zetterling, she's Swedish.'

Dad's eyes widened. 'Oh!' It turned out that Mai was one of his favourites, 'She was my pin-up!'

This was a relief to me because *if* I got the job he would have to sign my contract as I was under eighteen.

I was the most nervous I'd been in my life as I made my way to Soho's Berwick Street. I didn't know what I was supposed to do but Anna had said the first audition would probably just be a chat. And so it was.

Mai was beautiful and tiny. She'd been working as a leading film actress for many years but soon became bored and, after directing for a few more years, was now ready to take the helm of a British feature. She told me she'd seen me at one of Anna's classes but was worried about the no Equity card problem that myself and a few other people she liked were in. 'I'm trying to see if something can be done, but best not to get your hopes up.'

I went for two more auditions, the second of which involved a group of us telling stories and doing improvisations. I told the story of Steve in the detention centre and the piglet named Kath, which made everyone laugh.

And then came the eternal and insufferable waiting. I'd very nearly forgotten about it, not knowing how long these things took. We'd finally had a telephone installed at home. It only ever really rang for me or Carm. I answered when her dad eventually called after the six months' silence. A very deep, accented voice asked, 'May I speak with Carmelita, please? It's her father.'

I bolted up the stairs to her and Barry's bedroom, banging on the door with excitement. 'Carmy! Your dad's on the phone!'

The door flew open, tears already falling and words tumbling reminiscent of the film *The Railway Children*, 'Daddy! My daddy!' She rushed down the stairs and they talked, along with her mum, for over an hour. It was such a happy relief.

I eventually got a call from Sandra, Anna's assistant at the time. 'Anna needs you to come up to the office.'

'Have I got the part?' I nervously asked.

'I don't know,' she said (she did), 'you just have to come up today if you can.'

Anna greeted me with a hug. 'Darling, Kathy! I'm very happy to tell you that Mai Zetterling would like you to play the role of Glennis in *Scrubbers*. She's had a meeting with Equity and they're in agreement that, along with some other girls, you are to be given a temporary card for the duration of the job. This is very unusual so I'm relying on you to be extremely professional at all times. We will act as your agents and will take ten per cent of your earnings. Myself and Charles have also decided that, along with Elaine, you can now join the Friday professional class. Here's the script and the contract from HandMade Films, which your dad has to read carefully and sign because you're only seventeen. Well done! We're all so very proud of you!'

I hugged her back, holding tightly to stop myself from passing out.

AND SO IT BEGINS

'HANDMADE SCRUBBERS' was written on a piece of paper that was taped to the window of the coach we had to meet at King's Cross before dawn had even broken. It was taking us to the disused Holloway Sanatorium in Virginia Water, Surrey, which was our filming location. I'd never knowingly met a lesbian before and now lesbian-in-chiefess Miriam Margolyes, who was playing one of the borstal wardens, was announcing she was the Equity deputy and any problems or worries we were to go to her. She was as filthy-mouthed back then as she is today and I thought she was fabulous.

We were a ramshackle bunch and quite a lot of us had never acted professionally before. I was sick with nerves but felt better once I'd gleaned I wasn't the only newbie.

We had five days of rehearsals before filming started, so got to know each other pretty quickly. A new theatre company called Clean Break was helping imprisoned women with writing and acting workshops as part of a rehabilitation programme and some of our cast who had been in prison were now reaping the benefits. We also had the singer Dana Gillespie as our lead screw, and she entertained us with brilliant stories of debauchery from the '60s and '70s.

On the last rehearsal day, one of our executives from HandMade Films was popping in to say hello. It was George Harrison from The Beatles and I was gobsmacked. Mai wanted to make sure we all had a chance to meet him, so we formed an orderly queue to shake him by the hand. He was smiling as I approached, put out his beautiful hand and said shyly in his wonderful voice that I already knew so well, 'I feel like Prince Charles.'

I so wanted to reply, *You don't look like him, though!* But the words wouldn't come out, so I just giggled and mumbled, 'Yeah'.

I loved filming. The entire crew was male and could be quite salacious, but they were kind to me because I was one of the youngest and they thought I was funny. Mai hated the 'banter' and would give evil looks to anyone she felt was crossing a line. She wore a black two-piece karate suit every day to show her strength and now and then would whisper in my ear that men were pigs or weren't to be trusted. I found this strange as she had a boyfriend, so surely she trusted him? I was still beautifully naive.

My character, Glennis, had a few scenes but one I was worried about. I was supposed to be scared at someone shouting and screaming from another cell so was to get into bed with my cellmate, played by Faith Tingle, and have a cuddle that would lead to a kiss. A *kiss*? With *a girl*?! I didn't vocalise my fear, as I wanted to be professional, but I was absolutely shitting myself. When it came to it, though, Mai decided she no longer wanted this scene in the film and instead asked me to sit on my bunk and tell the story as if to the other inmates, of Steve and the pigs. I changed our names and happily told my true-life, self-deprecating tale, which made the final cut.

Another exec on the film was a guy called Ray. Only seventeen years older than me but at the age I was he seemed like any of the other *old* bald men knocking around. A big set piece of *Scrubbers* was a concert scene, our makeshift instruments being pots and pans that crescendoed with a girl chucking a potty of saved-up shit at an enemy. Nice. For some reason I always fancied myself as a bit of a drummer so volunteered to be the one opening the scene with a flat-handed drumroll on an upturned pot pretending to be a bongo drum. As we were rehearsing, Ray came over, trying to give me some tips. I was a bit affronted at this old bloke telling me what to do. 'Alright, mate! I know what I'm doing. No need to stick your oar in!' I had no clue he was actually Ray Cooper, one of the best percussionists in the country, working mostly alongside Elton John.

The worst thing about filming was missing my Friday evening lessons at Anna Scher's. When Elaine and I had started them a couple of months before, we knew we would need someone to help us get into the Edward pub next door to the theatre, as we were still underage. Everyone went there after the lesson and we didn't want to miss out. My dad had drunk in most of the pubs in Islington and had recently told me about a girl called Tilly who sometimes worked as a barmaid at the Old Red Lion pub on St John Street. *She* was in the Friday group and, 'I told her you were going there and she said she'd keep an eye out for you.'

I berated him once again for interfering but still passed his information on to Elaine. 'My dad says Tilly Vosburgh is a really nice girl so she'll probably let us go into the pub with her.'

The only time you were allowed to be late to a lesson was if you were working, so we worried about Tilly not being there but she turned up eventually after a day filming something and did a very funny improvisation about KitKats. She was one of a handful of middle-class students there, but we didn't hold that against her. She lived in one of the posher roads between Upper Street and Liverpool Road. Her mum Beryl had been an actress before having a brood of six, and her lovely American dad, Dick Vosburgh, was a very brilliant comedy sketch and West End musicals writer. Tilly herself was very sexy with a wide, inviting mouth and beautiful sea-green eyes. Elaine whispered in my ear, 'Oh my God, she's brilliant, let's definitely ask her to get us into the Edward!' So we did. There's been a couple of blips along the way but the three of us have remained firm friends ever since.

I cried on the last day of filming *Scrubbers*, giving big snotty hugs to my favourites Yelena, Rachel, Faith and Dawn. I'd had such a fantastic time and, as far as I knew, it would probably be my one and only professional acting job. Mai had been an invaluable influence. She told me I would eventually get bored with acting so should also think about writing or directing too. I thought this was madness as I couldn't even *imagine* getting bored. What on earth was she on about?! She also said she would like to meet my dad. *What?* I'd told her at some point that he was a fan and now she was asking if she could come to ours for a cup of tea. Nobody ever came to ours, especially not an international film star who had become a rare female director. Dad was mostly sober now so I broached the idea with him, rather than keep it to myself and pretend it never happened, which I would've done if he was still drinking.

On the day she was due to arrive Dad sent me to Chapel Market to buy some proper cups and saucers as we only had mugs. 'I don't think she'll be bothered about that,' I said, 'she's quite hippyfied.' But he insisted, so I did.

It was strange to see him shyly greet her. John was there too and we sat in the kitchen, drinking tea and eating cake that Dad also insisted I got from Marks & Spencer's. Then Mai turned to us and said, 'I'd like to talk with your dad on our own if that's okay? Pat, will you show me the garden?' Then she and Dad had a chat outside for an hour or so, and neither of them shared with me what was said till many years later.

What an extraordinary thing to have happened. I'm so glad Dad and John got to meet her.

Not long after the job finished, I received a little package from Equity containing a letter along with a provisional union card. Miriam had informed them that I was wholly professional during filming and a potential asset to the industry, and this was my reward. I was over the blooming moon! It meant I could carry on working as an actor and do my forty weeks till I got my full, official membership. I packed in college and did what every new actor starting out does: sat by the telephone and waited.

'HI-DIDDLE-DEE-DEE'

It took a few months but now aged eighteen I had finally got my first stage job, with a theatre-in-education company called Major Road, who were based in Bradford. The play, *Operation Elvis* by C.P. Taylor, told the story of a young man with cerebral palsy who is befriended by a non-disabled young man obsessed with Elvis Presley. I played the first young man's useless carer who was more interested in flirting with the Elvis character than looking after her charge. It was great fun. We toured schools and youth clubs all across Yorkshire, sometimes doing three shows a day, plus we had to put up and take down its flimsy set before and after each performance, hence our tour catchphrase 'Where's the fucking hammer?'

My close friends on the job were Alsie our company manager, Ian Sears (Elvis) and Andrew Paul (the young man with cerebral palsy). Ian and Andy both went to Anna Scher's but I only really got to know them on the tour. I *loved* Ian, he was so sweet and really funny but he was smitten with Tilly at the time, as were most of the boys, so another lifelong friendship was born instead.

We stayed in some awful digs that were all freezing cold with rattling windows. The landladies were hard as nails with strict 'No messing about!' rules. We would mimic them to each other, and the boys agreed that my accent was the best. I would put this to better use a few years later by creating a comedy character from Keighley.

When we'd finished a show we'd go to a pub then go back to the digs and I'd join the boys in their room. They'd introduced me to spliff, which I was totally uninterested in at first, 'Nah, you're alright, thanks, I'm happy with my lager.' But after a couple of weeks curiosity got the better of me and when I tried it I had the greatest feeling of relaxation that my catchphrase then became, 'Who's skinning up?'

Andy was very funny. He could play the piano out of tune like Les Dawson and would do a hilarious impression of a learner driver on empty stretches of motorway – which existed in the '80s.

While we were touring, *Scrubbers* was released. There was a press screening early one Monday morning in Leicester Square and Andy – who had been in *Scum* so was very curious – suggested we all go along and he could drive us back up north to wherever our venue was that evening.

It was very strange watching the film. It seemed so different from the script, and I of course was shocked at myself when I finally made an appearance. I was funny but, *Did I really talk like that?* And, *Why is my body that shape?* And, *Where are my fucking lips???*

We hovered outside the cinema after so I could have a smoke when an American voice said 'Hi Kathy!' It was Jack, my film studies tutor, with a man he didn't introduce.

'Jack!' I exclaimed, giving him a hug. 'What are you doing here?'

It turned out he had a side job writing film reviews for *Gay News* or *Capital Gay* (can't remember which). I could tell he wasn't overly impressed with the film, but it was still very nice to see him, and he wished me the best of luck with my career.

Andy gave his own disparaging review on the drive back. 'You come out of it okay but it's not a patch on *Scum*.' Then he did a bit of learner driver man to make me feel better.

He was right of course and a lot of the official reviews were in agreement. It was very deflating and I felt sad for Mai who had worked so hard and given so many of us a kickstart into the industry. Oh well, that's showbiz!

Ian was a middle-class, private-school-educated boy from Belsize Park, a very affluent area of north-west London. After we'd finished the tour we hung out together constantly. He had his own, very tasteful, one-bedroom flat with an incredibly spacious living room where we'd get stoned and listen to David Bowie and Prince records. He was a fantastic cook and would often make me dinner when I'd accepted an *invitation*. I was curious about how he could afford such an amazing gaff at such a young age. I knew he'd done some TV work but surely he couldn't have earned the sort of money that would lead to this amazing place so quickly? After some months he said he had an embarrassing confession to make. His dad owned a few properties and the flat was gifted to Ian on his eighteenth birthday. I thought this was amazing and didn't understand why he was embarrassed.

'Because your upbringing was a struggle and you didn't have any money and this place was just bloody *handed* to me!'

I let his mortification sink in then said, 'But you're *sharing* it with me, mate. You share everything with me and I think that's brilliant.'

He was relieved and I felt proud of him and his empathic spirit. I'm proud of myself, too, that even from a young age I never measured a person on what they did or didn't have. The working-class chip didn't exist on my shoulder as I'd already reaped the kindness of so many sharers, so who was I to judge?

ALWAYS MEET YOUR HEROES

The actress and singer Mandi Symonds, who had been in *Scrubbers*, rang me out of the blue. She was singing in a band with Simon Brint and Rowland Rivron that was part of a live touring show of *The Young Ones*, which was a massive cultural event on TV and had kicked off a whole new wave of alternative comedy, including *The Comic Strip Presents . . .* Its standout star was the hilariously brilliant Rik Mayall, whose comedy creations Rick the student and Kevin Turvey were already firm favourites across the country and with me.

Mandi said, 'A few of us went to see *Scrubbers* on a day off and Rik Mayall thinks you're great and really wants to meet you. We're playing in Wimbledon next week and a couple of the girls from the film are coming so do you fancy it? You won't have to pay, I can put your name on the door and you can meet Rik afterwards.'

I couldn't breathe. Was this really happening? Rik Mayall thought I was great?! What the fuckity fuck?! Of course I wanted to go. Just try and stop me!

The show was brilliant and totally chaotic. Everyone was hilarious, including Mandi and the band, but Rik was, of course, the best. When I went backstage afterwards, the chaos was continuing. Lots of people drinking lots of booze and shouting lots and lots. They were all a few years older than me so seemed very grown up and very brainy as most of them had been to university. It was a whole new world.

The man himself couldn't have been sweeter. 'Hello, Kath! Did you enjoy the show?! God, you were GREAT in *Scrubbers*!

You're VERY FUNNY! It's GREAT to meet you! We're going to the Comedy Store now to see Ben Elton and you HAVE to come!'

So we all piled into the tour bus and headed to Leicester Square. When we arrived, Rik grabbed me by my arm, 'Come with ME!' He led me to the box office at the bottom of the stairs and said to the guy in the booth, 'THIS young lady is VERY VERY FUNNY and I INSIST you give her a lifetime membership card because SHE will be a very funny person for a LIFETIME!' So he did, and the little blue and white card lived in my little Equity card wallet for years after.

There's no dialogue from me at this meeting because I honestly don't remember saying a single word back to him. I was dumbstruck.

TWO DARK CLOUDS

John got really sick. It was the beginning of kidney problems that would trouble him for years. When he first fell ill, the doc sent him to A&E, where he promptly passed out, so they sent him to Intensive Care. He'd very nearly died on us and it was absolutely terrifying.

I was by his bed when he woke and asked where Dad was.

'Outside in the corridor,' I said.

'Keep him there,' John said, 'I'm not in the mood for his tears.'

This was the thing about Dad we couldn't bear even more than his punches. He got highly emotional whenever we were sick, which felt weird and false as he didn't seem to give a shit the rest of the time. When Barry started to have epileptic seizures, Dad would curl up in bed with the blankets over his head and John would have to deal with them. Dad was the child of the family and by the time we got older we no longer had the patience for it.

However, there were a couple of very dark times when he became an able man. When John was finally sent home after the long spell in hospital, he said Dad was pretty good and stayed sober during his longer recovery at home, taking over the cooking and cleaning. John got very low-spirited, which was understandable especially as he was still so young and finally getting to enjoy life, so it was a strange feeling of relief that Dad was around. I was out the door for as much as possible by then so wasn't much help myself.

Barry and Carm had finally got their own place, miles away in the basement flat of the house slap bang next door to ours.

I loved popping in for a cuppa and a smoke with Carm, Marvin Gaye's *What's Going On* a constant on the turntable. She was great fun and the pair of us were always laughing about something with Barry rolling his eyes at our stupidity but smirking all the while.

A few years into their marriage, Barry was working as a manager at Royal Mail's headquarters and Carm was in recruitment. They'd taken themselves off for a skiing holiday in Andorra, but the worst thing happened while they were away. Carm's dad rang the house and spoke with my dad for ages. Carm's younger brother had had a terrible accident and was on life support in hospital. Back then, there was no way of getting in touch with people when they were abroad. We didn't even know what airport they were flying into. Carm's dad wanted to make sure she didn't find out from messages on their phone answering machine and asked Dad to please tell her what had happened himself and to call him the moment she arrived home.

On the morning they were due back Dad paced around by the front-room window until he saw a taxi approaching. 'God help me now while I break that little girl's heart.' He went out to them and I watched from the window, too frightened to go outside myself. The look on Carm's face was heartbreaking as she dropped her case and ran into their flat to make the call.

After an awful couple of weeks when Carm and her family kept vigil by the hospital bed, we heard the devastating news that her brother had passed away, and the subsequent depression that engulfed her would stay with Carm for the rest of her life.

A HARD TRUTH

It was becoming apparent that not everyone in the industry felt the same way about me as Anna Scher did. When a director or casting director got in touch looking for 'a young beauty' she would often put me forward along with the pretty girls as she felt I was such a good actor my 'inner beauty would shine through'. It didn't. I was often met with a startled look as I walked through the door of an audition and it was starting to get to me. In the end I had to ask her to just put me up for unusual or funny or real-looking characters to help make the process less painful. I wasn't a leading lady and didn't ever expect to be.

I did a few good jobs, but I was so spoiled by the love and attention I had on *Scrubbers* and *Operation Elvis* that for the most part they were pretty unsatisfying to play. I was usually a fat mate of an attractive girl or a thick fuck among a crowd of whatever, and unless the writing was great and gave my character more than a couple of clichéd lines, they all merged into one. The money could be good, though, and claiming the dole in between was less of a hassle back then.

A couple of good jobs involving good people stand out. A director called Colin Bucksey really liked me after I did a small part for him in the kids' TV show *Educating Marmalade*, which starred the wonderful Charlotte Coleman. He liked my improvisations and kept a couple of tiny bits in the final cut. There was a good-looking older actor on the show who was a bit pervy with us younger ones. He hassled me one time during lunch, asking if I was enjoying my sex life and he could help with it if I wasn't, etc. I didn't really know what to say, so just laughed along with him but another actor, Zoot Money, who was also a musician, told him to shut up then turned to me and said, 'This guy's a fucking idiot, don't indulge him or any of the other fucking idiots you're bound to come across. Stick with boys your own age.' What a darling.

The actress playing Marmalade's mum was the brilliantly funny Lynda Marchal. One day she gave me a lift home and as we were chatting I told her I'd quite like to try writing at some point. 'That's a great idea,' she said, puffing on a cigarette as she wove through the traffic. 'I've written something myself actually that starts filming soon. If it goes well I'll give up this acting lark and write full-time.' I was surprised. She was such a fantastic actress, would she really stop completely? 'God, yes!' she exclaimed with a throaty laugh. 'That's the dream, kid!' Her dream became a reality. Her pen name is Lynda La Plante, her show was the award-winning *Widows* and she continued to write with huge success, most notably the universal smash hit *Prime Suspect* starring Helen Mirren. What a genius.

Colin asked for me again when he was directing a TV play set in the eighteenth century (can't remember what it was called), starring Donald Pleasence who had been a film star for many years doing standout supporting roles. I had two tiny parts in that, a prostitute and a pie seller: 'Pies, all hot, hot, hot!' When I finished filming, Mr Pleasence came to find me in Make-up to tell me he thought I was very talented and it wouldn't be easy for me in the industry but to never lose heart and to keep going. What a lovely bloke.

Another job I did during this post-*Scrubbers* period was a hard-hitting four-part drama about the state of the NHS. I played a very small role in an episode that focused on mental health. My character, a patient, was a sad little creature who was being molested by a male hospital porter under the guise of love. The director Les Blair was very good and I liked him – but during a scene where my character spots her abuser in the company of others and starts inappropriately vocalising her want for 'love', he asked if I could start touching myself on the you-know-where before I'm dragged away by the other staff members. I was shocked. It wasn't in the script, and I really didn't want to do it, so I simply said 'No'. Les was surprised at my refusal but thankfully was decent enough not to push it. What a relief for him now.

DRUNK II

I spent most of the mid- to late '80s pissed. Not while I was working, of course, and I wasn't a daytime drinker in general. On the rare occasions I did succumb to a day tipple, usually at some celebration or other, it gave me such a horrible feeling, akin to jet lag, that I avoided it when I could. But I did drink most evenings. A lot. Because it helped me sleep.

I was around nineteen when a little gang of us started going to the Old Red Lion (where Tilly sometimes worked), run by the strict but jovial Tony and the formidable Pauline. One of London's earliest fringe theatres was in a room above with about fifty or so seats. The first play I saw there or anywhere live was written and directed by the actor Phil Davis, who'd been in the films *Quadrophenia* and *Scum*. I approached him afterwards to ask how he'd gone about putting on the play, as Mai's earlier horse-whispering had sparked an interest and Lynda's car journey encouragement even more so. Phil was lovely and forthcoming with his advice, 'You just need to find a producer to help raise the funds, most of which is for renting the space. You'll probably come across a few brick walls trying to block your way, especially as you're a girl, but I'd advise anyone to give it a go as it's good fun and extremely rewarding. Much better than just being the puppet.'

I put that in my pocket for a few years and got on with being a 'jobbing actor', which was ironic as the jobs were few and far between.

Tilly, Elaine and I had become friends with Michèle Winstanley, Perry Fenwick, Steve Sweeney, David John and Wayne 'Pickles'

Norman to name a few, and Friday nights at the Old Red were becoming a regular occurrence.

Michael was now going steady so I didn't see him as much any more but we are still friends, and Ange? Ange had fallen in love with a Norwegian guy on holiday, married him and moved to Norway. Some years later on a sporadic phone catch-up she proudly told me, 'My kids ski to school, Kaf!'

My closest friend from the new crowd was Perry (also known as 'Pelso') who grew up in East Ham with his close-knit family. Perry loved a natter, pinning me down for a cuddle and the band Madness. He'd already done a fair bit of acting work since he was a teenager and I'd seen him be fantastic in a *Play for Today* on the telly and a film by the incredibly talented actor Daniel Peacock called *Party Party*. Perry introduced me to Daniel when he was casting for his short film *Espresso Splasho*, and I ended up with a small but nice part in it thanks to Pel.

Tilly and Elaine were getting more acting jobs than me so I started working as a barmaid at the Old Red but mostly during the lunchtime shifts as I found the evenings too much to bear. It wasn't people being drunker in the evenings I couldn't handle, it was me not being able to be drunk with them.

Pauline would beg me to 'put a bit of lipstick on' as even back then I hated wearing make-up. It made my skin itch. Mascara and a bit of eyeliner was the most I'd do, lippy was a no-no. I knew I looked better with it because, let's be honest, who doesn't? I just didn't like the *feel* of it. However, knowing it bothered old-school Pauline and because I did really like her, I'd bung a bit on for my shifts, using garish colours such as nude.

It was much more of a drinking culture back then and the people, mostly men, who worked nearby would pop in for one, but generally two or three lunchtime pints and maybe a spirit chaser just to get them ready for an afternoon's graft. I was glad I wasn't conventionally pretty. Pretty barmaids like regular Maria had to put up with a barrage of sexual innuendo, but I only suffered this if some perv just liked them young. My stock answer to 'Give us a smile, darling!' was 'Give me five pounds.' Or, 'Do you fancy coming out with me tonight?' would be met with 'Can't, I'll be busy washing you from my memory.' Or for anything too salacious a simple 'Fuck off' would suffice. Pauline would give me a poke with a beautifully manicured finger and growl under a fixed smile, 'You can't talk to the customers like that!' She mustn't have really minded, though, because she never sacked me.

The evenings, when I was a customer, were great fun, particularly on a Friday when everyone would turn up. If I or any of the others befriended someone on a job we'd tell them Friday night at the Old Red was the place to be, and over time our little mob grew and grew and grew. We had the Manchester gang, the Scousers, the Normals (people who didn't work in the industry) and the Kids (people from Anna's who were younger than us who we made sit at a different table). Plus future Doctor Who, Jo Martin, her make-up artist sister Sharon and on the odd occasion Tim Roth and Daniel Day-Lewis.

I was semi-responsible for the Scottish contingent, having worked on an episode of a great comedy show with John Gordon Sinclair called *No Problem!* starring the brilliant Victor Romero Evans. Gordie, who was famous for being the lead in cult classic *Gregory's Girl*, complained that he hadn't yet found a good pub in London so I told him about the Old Red. In he came the next week with a fantastic gang of folk who were mostly actors, artists and musicians. They were cool and funny, particularly Fraser Taylor, Caroline Guthrie, Brian Bolger, Peter Capaldi (another future Doctor Who) and his then-girlfriend (and now-wife) Elaine Collins, and a quietly spoken bloke, Kenny McClymont, who was renamed Whispering Ken.

Pauline also got me involved with the ladies' darts team at the Old Red, as she suspected I'd be good at it. She was right. I wasn't too handy at pool, though, and it took months of humiliating practice before I won a game. I was greeted with a banner the next day, made by Tony, which read, 'KATHY WON A GAME OF POOL!'

There were occasional charity events that I was asked to 'host', which was basically just me standing on the pool table shouting out raffle ticket winners and taking the piss out of the regulars. It was good practice for the stand-up comedy act I never pursued.

The best thing about the Friday nights, though, were the lock-ins. We could be in there till two, three in the morning, completely splattered, with Tony giving out free sandwiches midway to help soak up the booze. We'd laugh, sing, cry, fight, make up and look forward to doing it all again the following week.

ADVISER

Tilly had gained the highly envious job of working with the director Mike Leigh on a film he would eventually call *Meantime*. His way of working is too complex for me to explain here, but in simple terms the characters are found from a list of candidates from real life supplied by the actors. The cast then work together on improvisations, which Mike eventually weaves and structures into the story. Everything is top-secret so the cast didn't talk to anyone outside of the project about it. It was panning out, though, that some of the characters were going to be skinheads and Tilly mentioned to Mike that one of her friends used to be one. Me. There's always extensive research required so Mike asked Tilly if I would come in and give a little talk as part of this, so I did.

I was a bit sick with nerves beforehand, as Mike was already a big deal in the industry, having made the TV plays *Bleak Moments*, *Abigail's Party* and *Nuts in May*. I gave my talk to Tilly, Mike and a handful of cast members – which reminded me of my failed oral English exam in school – and then answered a few questions. I was there for less than two hours and earned thirty pounds, which I was really chuffed with.

When the film was finished, Mike invited me to a small screening and I thought it was fantastic. One of the cast members who was at my talk took a shine to me and a year or so later would suggest me for a play he was going to star in at a repertory theatre in Westcliff-on-Sea. His name was Gary Oldman.

CHANGES IN TASTE

I was no longer spending my money on gigs. I was still really into music, but by now Tilly had introduced me to Ella Fitzgerald, Billie Holiday and, my new favourite, Nina Simone, so I was collecting their albums and going to the theatre instead. The West End was beyond my price range but there were plenty of fringe theatres to attend and other affordable places like the Theatre Royal Stratford East. I saw so much great stuff and quite a lot of crap. If a mate was in something I would sometimes be given a comp, but this was pretty rare. The most stuff I saw was at the Old Red as it was very handy to get to, what with it being upstairs from where I drank, and Richard Hansom – who was its artistic director at the time – would often let me sneak in for free. I was in about three plays there myself, two with Tilly, which was great fun and good experience, but they never really led to much apart from making my CV look less empty, and I was starting to get a little frustrated. Don't get me wrong, I loved living the creative life, but a little more consistency would have been nice.

I attempted to write something, encouraged by Perry, but it was pretty bad so I took it no further than an exercise in discipline.

The play I was in with Gary Oldman, *Saved* by Edward Bond, was a controversial piece written and set in the '60s. Gary would be in another production at the Royal Court Theatre in London about a year later, but our production was directed by Di Trevis at the Palace Theatre in Westcliff. Caroline Quentin was its lead girl, Pam, playing opposite Gary's character, Len, and my role was Liz, whose significance was minor. It was great to be working *and* working away from home as I found myself back in cold digs that I shared with Gary and a couple of other cast members, which was a laugh. The play itself was great and Gary mesmerising to watch but after a while I was getting bored out of my mind playing a role that appeared towards the end of a three-hour play where she did nothing much except ask for a coffee. 'There are no small parts only small actors' was another of Anna Scher's mantras that I kept in my head as I stepped out on to the stage each night and every empty auditorium matinee but it didn't really help my disheartenment.

Tilly and Elaine were getting some good theatre jobs that were always brilliant fun to go to. They were such great actors so even if the plays were rubbish, trudging here, there and everywhere to see them was never a chore.

The first time I went to the Edinburgh Fringe was to see Tilly in an enjoyable play called *Johnny Oil Strikes Back*. Elaine and I could only afford to stay a few nights but we managed to cram loads in, as cheaply priced plays, cabaret and stand-up comedy were available to see all day, every day. Norman Lovett was a standout favourite and of course *Johnny Oil*, which we saw twice. Tilly met her partner, Ade, on that Edinburgh job and two kids and over forty years later they are still together today.

It was around this time I stopped eating meat. It wasn't a conscious decision, I just couldn't stomach it any more. All those lovely sausages and steak and kidney pies of my childhood were becoming a distant memory and as there weren't the choices we have today, baked potatoes with various veggie toppings became my staple instead. There was a restaurant in Camden Passage called Serendipity that we would frequent if we had the money. They did a great broccoli, cheesy pasta dish that I'd have with garlic bread. A small gang of us went there for my twenty-first birthday along with John and, fanfare please, a very sober Dad. John recalls Dad being quite nervous and asking John to order for him. It was the first and only time the three of us ate out together.

Away from theatre I finally landed a nice role in a film for Channel 4 called *Sacred Hearts*. Set in a convent school during the Second World War, it starred Katrin Cartlidge, Oona Kirsch and Anna Massey, who was famous for being in Alfred Hitchcock's *Frenzy*. My part was small but I was in the background of lots of scenes so got paid pretty well. My bad teeth were definitely a factor in not getting certain jobs so I decided it was about time to face the dreaded dentist and finally get the old choppers fixed. *That* was what I was going to spend the money on. However . . .

HEY, MISS PRODUCER!

Robert Pugh, a brilliant Welsh actor, writer and director, was already a bit of a legend at the Old Red before my time there. He'd written and directed a couple of plays for upstairs but the one I saw was a surreal and hilarious piece called *How Grim Was My Alley*. Bob was a working-class maverick – which was a rarity in the industry – and was mostly known for turning down great work in order to pursue the pleasures of life such as golf and women. He was very sexy and extremely funny.

I'd met him briefly a couple of times up the Old Red and he was always great craic, but on one particular occasion he was grumpy and frustrated. The rent for the theatre space upstairs had gone up, meaning he didn't have enough funds for his next project, around two grand.

I'd been working upstairs now and then in a backstage capacity, running the box office and a bit of stage management, more for learning than for money (as there wasn't any) but really wanted to work as an assistant director, a role that was rare on the fringe as it was seen as another expense and therefore a bit of a luxury.

Bob had written a new one-act play for two actors called *Therapy*. He was to star and direct but was now in a pickle as his main money person had dropped out because of the rent hike. I listened to his woes then found myself saying, 'As you're going to be in it you'll be *needing* an assistant director, so I'll give you the money if you let me assist.' I hadn't even read the play but had witnessed his skills so hoped it was worth the risk. Bob said yes.

My gamble paid off because the play was brilliant and

completely ahead of its time, but if you were to talk to Bob himself about the experience all he would tell you is that one day during a line run I was lying down. He quite rightly snapped when I did this, but I always found it a wind-up that he wouldn't tell people my other contributions to the production, as well as paying for the bloody thing, so it's nice to put down the facts of the matter now.

The play takes place during a therapy session in a psychiatric hospital between a white-coat-wearing, pompous psychiatrist (Bob) and a younger Black male patient. A battle of minds and words ensues with Bob's sharp and witty dialogue. Then, around halfway through, we learn that who we thought was the patient is actually the shrink and what we've been witnessing is a session of role play. It was always a thrill to be in the audience when the revelation occurred, a quiet unified gasp when the actual doctor asks for his white coat back.

Bob had a few actors in mind to play the actual doctor but none were available so I brought my friend Treva Etienne in for an audition. He always carried himself with an air of mature sophistication so I thought he'd be great. Treva was far too young for the part as he was only around twenty-three at the time and the character was down as being thirty, but I asked him to come in a bit early so I could have a sly word before Bob turned up, 'Trev, I know you'd be brilliant in the role but Bob might think you're too young so just lie and say you're late twenties.'

Treva wasn't too sure. 'I don't know, Kath, the play is great and I love the part but I don't know if he'd believe me.'

'Just *act* older,' I said, 'and put your youthfulness down to good genes. He won't question it if you're confident, and you do *look* like a doctor.'

Treva laughed and nodded. 'I hear you, I hear you.'

He got the job.

When it came to the music, Bob was insistent he didn't want to use a known classical piece to open and underscore the play, even though it wouldn't cost me, its producer, anything, but he wanted an original composition on the cello. The only problem being he didn't know any cellists. Fortunately, I did. Màrius Díaz Lleal was studying music in London and was sharing a flat with Nick Conway, who was in *Johnny Oil* with Tilly and the brother of her boyfriend Ade. I'd met Màrius a few times and he'd often impress us with his musicality when having late-into-the-night drinking sessions back at their flat. I brought him in to meet and play for Bob, who was blown away, so he too got the job. Màrius's composition was dark and beautiful, leading Bob to say it was like a third character in the play.

It was a good rehearsal period, apart from that one time I lay down of course, and I learned a great deal from Bob, particularly light and sound plotting and how to stay alert during the boring bits. Treva was wonderful as the doctor, and I don't recall anyone questioning his age.

We did a sell-out three-week run, which meant everyone got paid through the box office split, then a fringe theatre festival in Amsterdam *paid us* to take it there for another two-week run. Bob wound me up on the ferry going over, telling me there was a room with a pool table on one of the upper decks. I trudged around searching for ages until it dawned on me as I stumbled in a sway that we were on a fucking boat. I found Bob and Treva in a bar laughing their heads off at my gullibility.

We had a great time in Amsterdam, frequenting the dope cafes and eating chips with mayonnaise. The play itself was again a sell-out so I eventually got back all the money I'd invested and a bit extra on top. I actually made quite a bit more money than Bob, which irked him somewhat, but I think he was proud of me deep down.

Treva and I also told Bob Trev's real age on the ferry taking us home after the successful Amsterdam run. His face was a picture, 'You lying bastards!' It was a very happy and very fulfilling experience.

DINNER INVITES

My friend Michèle Winstanley was a very attractive and very artistic actress living round the corner from the big house in the same now-converted flat that the Rileys from my childhood had lived in. It was nicely odd to be back in my old extra-breakfast domain. Mich is one of those creative people who can turn their hand to blooming anything – writing, painting, knitting and the like. She also decorated the flat herself and could change plugs. I marvelled at her efficiency. In later life she qualified as a sign language interpreter and told me about a time she spotted a couple of people signing to each other on a bus. Tickled pink with her new qualification, she approached and signed to them about her knowledge, to which one signed back, 'Well done but kindly fuck off as we're having a private conversation.'

Mich would sometimes drive us to the Fletchers' in Palmers Green in her VW Beetle Bug. Big Steve and Wendy Fletcher had been chaperones before my time at Anna Scher's and had three actor sons: Little Steve, Graham and the already famous Dexter. Mich was treated like the daughter they didn't have and I was welcomed with open arms. Big Steve was a brilliant cook but I remember thinking the first time I went, *Oh shit, I thought we were having dinner.* I could smell something lovely but there was no sign of any cooking when we were sitting in their spotless kitchen. Then, much to my relief, out from the oven came a magnificent veggie lasagne along with a huge bowl of crunchy green salad from the fridge. 'How come there's no mess after you made all this?' I asked.

Big Steve laughed, saying, 'It's all about the prep, love, and I clean as I go.'

He was always telling me I should write. After the feasting he would take us into the living room to watch Pinter plays he'd recorded from the telly or we'd listen to Miles Davis as he and Wendy told stories about their younger days when they were hipsters in London's swinging jazz club scene. It was always a lovely time, and to this day whenever I'm prepping a meal for friends I clean as I go and I think of Big Steve.

THE COX TRILOGY

I had an audition with director Alex Cox for a film he was making called *Sid and Nancy*, about Sid Vicious and Nancy Spungen's doomed love affair during and after Sid V's involvement with the Sex Pistols. Alex said he'd wanted to work with me since seeing *Scrubbers* and offered the part of Brenda Windzor, one of the Pistols' entourage, while I was still in the room. I was over the bleeding moon and even more so when he told me he'd offered the part of Sid to Gary Oldman.

The gorgeous Chloe Webb was playing Nancy, Andrew Schofield was Johnny Rotten and two great actors from Anna Scher's, Tony London and Perry Benson, were Steve Jones and Paul Cook. The rest of the entourage included my already friends Michèle Winstanley, Graham Fletcher, Mark Monero and Sara Sugarman, and its director of photography was the then relatively unknown Roger Deakins.

Alex wanted my character to have bleach-blonde hair so I spent a painful few hours in a grungy salon in Kensington Market before filming began. It looked okay punked-up but dreadful flat, much like Myra Hindley.

We had a weird rehearsal period where Alex got a few of us to read John Webster's *The Duchess of Malfi*. I didn't understand a fucking word of it but pretended I did.

Filming was a riot. It felt strange and wonderful to act out scenes of real-life events that I was too young to take part in at the time. A favourite couple of days was shooting a scene where the band do an illegal gig on a boat on the Thames during the Queen's Jubilee. I had great fun 'fighting' with supporting artists playing the police who stormed the boat when it docked.

I enjoyed the film when I saw it. I thought Gary and Chloe were excellent and some of Roger Deakins's photography, particularly in the film's second half, was stunning. I didn't watch myself as I'd now started to close my eyes whenever I appeared in anything. I'd become very self-critical about my acting and this only led to frustration as there was nothing I could do about it once something was already on the screen, so I decided early on: best not to watch.

The next film with Alex took us to Almería in Spain.

Straight to Hell was a homage to Sergio Leone's spaghetti westerns. It was written by Alex and his pal Dick Rude in under a week and shot in under a month. You could tell.

It was a mess to watch, but partly fun to make. Michèle was in it too so it was nice to have a mate around, and the rest of the cast was like a roll-call of that era's music and indie film establishment. It included: Elvis Costello and his partner at the time Cait O'Riordan, Jim Jarmusch, the entirety of The Pogues including their manager Frank Murray, Sy Richardson, Miguel Sandoval, Courtney Love, Grace Jones, Dennis Hopper and Joe Strummer, who had no recollection of my monumental life moment some years earlier. And why would he?

I hated the actual filming. Alex was like a madman. He was either shouting and sacking people left, right and centre or allowing indulgent and rubbish improvisations that felt like they went on for fucking days. I'm all for a bit of anarchy but it was too drug-induced and out of control for my liking. I was much happier on days off, when I could swim in the hotel pool and knock around with the wives and families of the cast and crew who had joined them for the jolly. I was especially fond of Marcia Farquhar, artist and wife of Jem Finer (Pogues), her two little kids Ella and Kitty and Jem's fabulous teacher sister Jess. Marcia was hilariously funny and scathing about the debauchery taking place around us. I also became close to James Fearnly (Pogues), who at the end of a day's filming liked to go off for quiet walks and meals away from the chaos and asked one time if I wanted to join him. I did, and it became our regular, peaceful ritual. I still see Marcia and Jem, and James whenever he's in London.

I didn't like Shane MacGowan much. Yes, he was a genius and I loved his songs as much as anyone, but I found his erratic personality difficult. He never called me by my name, instead he'd greet me with, 'Alright, stupid?'

To which I would respond, 'Yes, thanks for asking, prick.'

I loved the booze, I was still drinking on the regular and would often get lairy, but his intake was too much for me, it reminded me of Dad at his worst so I mostly steered clear.

Courtney Love was incredibly sweet. She'd come out with offbeat comments, shouting things like 'I feel like a fucking fish!' from nowhere. On mornings off she'd come to my room and ask me to order breakfast. We'd sit and chat and she'd eat a segment of orange or a bite of an apple, never eating the whole thing, like Jean Harlow in old films but with fruit instead of chocolate. It was only when I got my hotel bill at the end of the shoot I realised why we were always in my room and not hers.

One morning while getting ready in the unisex costume tent, I found myself alone with Elvis Costello, who was strumming something on a little acoustic guitar his character carried around.

I piped up, 'Give us a song, please,' and he obliged by singing the opening of 'I Want You' from his forthcoming album *Blood & Chocolate*. The first Friday after we finished filming, the majority of the cast came to the Old Red and Elvis gifted me a hot-off-the-press copy of the album.

You'd think I would have loved the craziness of it all but I really didn't and when Alex asked me to join him on his next movie I originally said thank you but no. The film was called *Walker* and would be shooting on location in Nicaragua for a couple of months. *Nicaragua?!* This was a country that was in the middle of a civil war between the Sandinista government and Contra rebels, the rebels being the bad guys who were funded and trained by Ronald Reagan's bully boys. William Walker was a real-life filibuster who invaded then declared himself president of Nicaragua in 1856, so it wasn't hard to decipher who Alex was having a dig at with this movie.

Alex took me for dinner at a rare-for-the-time Mexican restaurant in Covent Garden to introduce me to the abundance of veggie food choices that Latin America had to offer in the hope of persuading me to do the film. I told him bluntly that I didn't like working with him on *Straight to Hell* and was worried about being trapped in a country so far away from home if he was going to behave like a prick again. He was just as straightforward with his reply in his lovely, twisted Scouse-Atlantic accent, 'Almería was a different kettle of fish. I wanted to have a rock and roll adventure, taking drugs and sleeping with beautiful women, but this shoot won't be like that. I love the people of Nicaragua and they're going through far too much at the moment for me to take the piss. They're important to me and so is this movie. Almería was a fucked-up holiday. This is more serious.' I still wasn't convinced but said I'd think about it.

It was difficult before internet search engines to do much research, but I'd spotted in *Time Out* magazine that actress and political activist Charlotte Cornwell would be interviewing pre-fatwa Salman Rushdie about a book he'd written on his travels in Nicaragua, *The Jaguar Smile*, at the ICA on The Mall, so I got myself a ticket. It was all a bit highbrow for me, I didn't know what the fuck they were talking about so it wasn't helping with my decision, but I hovered around afterwards, bravely introduced myself to Charlotte and asked if I could have a quick chat with her. She very kindly obliged and we sat with a cuppa and a smoke while I told her my predicament.

'So what you're telling me,' she said with a kind air of puzzlement, 'is you've been offered a lifetime opportunity to go to a beautiful country *for free* to be in a film that you will be paid for and will also be looked after and protected?'

'Er, yes,' I meekly replied, 'but there is a war going on and Alex is a nutter, although he said he isn't any more, and my dad's worried I might get killed.'

To which she simply said, 'If you don't go I think you'll regret it for the rest of your life.'

So I went.

There was a handful of us from England including the brilliant Scottish actor David Hayman who had played Malcolm McLaren in *Sid and Nancy*, Spider Stacy (Pogues), Edward Tudor-Pole and Joe Strummer. The rest of the cast were mostly American and Mexican. Ed Harris played William Walker and was brilliant to watch as my part was tiny so I never got to act *with* him. My character, Annie Mae (I had to google it), was part of an army of twenty or so mercenaries Walker had cobbled together, with myself and American actress Sharon Barr being the only women.

A gang of us were put up at the InterContinental Hotel in Managua – I didn't know any of them – and everyone else was in Granada, where the majority of the film was shot. It was about an hour's drive, along one main road, from the hotel to the location and on day one a guide happily informed us, 'This is the most bombed road in Nicaragua!'

Alex was true to his word and ran the ship as tight as possible.

He still let improvisations go on for too long, though. The American actors loved the sound of their own voices but I'd learned to self-edit by then so hardly said a thing.

Michèle was there but not as an actor. She and another girl, Jo, took it in turns to take the rushes back to London a few times over the course of the filming so we didn't see that much of each other.

My close friends on the job were Sharon Barr, Xander Berkeley – who was also in *Sid and Nancy* and *Straight to Hell* – and an Egyptian-born, USA-based actor called René Assa who played a crazy doctor. René was wonderful, really knowledgeable and extremely good-humoured. He was already a great friend of Ed Harris's and the two of them taught me how to play poker with the bundles of córdobas we accumulated from our daily expenses.

The nights in the hotel could be a little nerve-wracking if there was fighting nearby. All the lights would shut off, making the sound of distant bombs and rattling machine guns even clearer. It was a relief when Van Morrison's *Astral Weeks* would start playing again on the portable ghetto blaster I'd brought from home, easing me back into a fitful sleep.

The Nicaraguan people I came across were beautiful and friendly. On night shoots young Sandinista cadets would guard the set. If they asked me where I was from, I would always say Ireland. Thatcher, along with Reagan, was loathed in these parts, so saying I was Irish was a short cut to solidarity.

One time there were more guards than usual, which puzzled me, until a bloke driving an open-top jeep turned up, surrounded by soldiers. He got out, greeted Alex and Ed with a hug and a slap to their backs, chatted, smiled and nodded for a bit, then jumped back into his jeep, and as he drove away the cadets cheered him off. It was Daniel Ortega, the country's president.

We spent a couple of days filming by the Pacific coast, I can't remember where exactly but, wherever it was, to describe it as breathtakingly beautiful would be an understatement. It was mesmerising. I was missing home of course, and my pals, and toast, but was very much enjoying the whole experience, until a very lonely couple of days.

One morning our bus to the location was pretty empty, as only a few of us were needed for whatever scene we were shooting. Ed Harris didn't have his own car like the star of a movie usually would. He wanted to muck in with the rest of us as the budget was low, and special treatment in poverty-stricken surroundings wouldn't have looked good, so he would sit up the front of the bus with the driver. However, on this roomy bus day, about halfway through the shoot, he was understandably grumpy and tired and didn't want to let on a group of locals who were helping our regular crew with odd jobs. The bus could get really hot when full so I got where he was coming from, especially as he was the one doing the most graft, but when I looked behind me (as I always sat at the back) I could see the crew bus was packed and the local guys were standing up. I expressed my concerns but was shut down by Ed calling over his shoulder, 'I wanna get going!'

Then a couple of boot-licking, method-acting Americans jumped in, 'Butt out! Ed needs space!'

I was shocked, particularly by one fat twat who was lying down, hungover, across two seats. 'You've got two seats, though! It's embarrassing!'

But again I was told to, 'Shut the fuck up, kid! This has nothing to do with you!'

The doors hissed closed once Ed told the driver to go, and I remained shocked and quiet at the back.

The day at work dragged as I kept to myself, reading a book between set-ups, then the journey back to the hotel was more quiet than usual and I noticed nobody was sitting with me. When we arrived, René took me to one side in the hotel lobby, 'Listen, sweetheart, I don't think you should join us in the poker game tonight, some of the guys are pretty mad at you because of this morning.'

I was shocked all over again. 'But all I said was we had room!'

'I know, I know,' he replied sympathetically, 'but best let the dust settle. I'll see you in the morning.'

I couldn't believe it. I was twenty-two and I had been 'sent to Coventry' in fucking Nicaragua! That evening dragged even longer as I stayed in my room, eating crisps from the dollar store while quietly sniffling with Van the Man.

I thought everything would be okay the next morning, but apart from René and Ed nobody said a word to me, so when we arrived on set I went up to Alex, said I wanted to go home and could I be booked on the next flight please. He was a bit taken aback and asked if I could wait until lunchtime when he'd be free to chat.

Over lunch I told him what had happened, adding, 'Those selfish, method-acting wankers think we're in a real army! I was mortified when I saw how full the other bus was. Anyway, I'm only in the background of the film so you won't miss me.' But Alex said he would miss me a lot as my integrity was one of the reasons he wanted me there in the first place, which surprised me as I always felt like I was a pain in his arse. He asked me to hold tight and promised to sort it out.

That evening, before our bus pulled out of the location parking area, Alex jumped on and gave a very clever speech. He thanked us all for our efforts so far, working in such a hot environment and so far away from home, but he also wanted to remind us why we were all there.

'Sure, we're making a movie but we're also helping the local community by giving people work and regular meals, which some haven't had for a *long* time. They're happy we're here so let's keep up the good work, good spirits and generosity.'

Everyone whooped and clapped as he jumped back off. The doors hissed closed and you could hear a pin drop. Alex hadn't mentioned what had happened, but we all knew what he was referring to. Then Ed stood up and in front of everyone called down to me and said, 'Sorry about the other day, Kathy.'

'That's alright,' I mumbled back, feeling a bit embarrassed but mightily relieved. The fat two-seat twat tried to apologise too but I knew he didn't mean it and was just following Ed's lead so I told him to go fuck himself.

For the last few weeks I moved from the hotel and into a house with Sharon, Xander and a couple of others who'd previously been staying in Granada. The house was lovely and homely and full of scampering geckos. I missed playing poker with René and Ed and hanging out with a young waiter I'd befriended called Berilo, who I nicknamed Pad, but still knocked around with René as much as I could during the day.

After more than eight weeks my journey home was interesting. We did a quick stop in El Salvador – which at the time was one of the most dangerous places on earth, then on to Mexico City, where I stayed in a room on the top floor of a high-rise hotel that felt like it swayed through the night, then, when I reached New York I wasn't allowed to leave the airport because I'd been in Nicaragua (traitor!) so spent five hours in JFK twiddling my sun-kissed thumbs. I was more than relieved when I was finally home, sat at our kitchen table in my beloved Islington with a mug of tea and a pile of toast, telling John and Dad all about my adventures.

The film unfortunately wasn't a success on release, which made me sad for Ed and especially Alex, who had worked so blooming hard, but it still felt good to send a thank-you-and-no-regrets card to Charlotte Cornwell.

POINTS OF VIEW

I've done many voice-overs for adverts over the years but the only time I appeared in one was in 1986. Directed by Paul Weiland for the *Guardian* newspaper and shot in grainy black and white, it shows a skinhead grappling with a businessman who we assume he's trying to rob. But then we're shown the event from a different perspective and what we see, when given the whole picture, is the skinhead was actually saving the businessman from some falling scaffolding. I played a young woman standing in a doorway. It was a well-paid day's filming and the advert itself is still to be found in the occasional top-ten-greatest-ads-ever polls. Classy.

A PECULIAR INTEREST

Life as an actor between jobs could be tedious and frustrating, never mind the added stress of being skint. The money from TV and film work was good but only lasted so long. Signing on the dole or working cash in hand at the pub helped, and if someone from the Old Red was doing a lucrative job they would help with a loan and vice versa, but I knew I had to get off my arse and create something myself if I wanted to move my career along.

Back in the '80s it wasn't the norm for actors to write and direct, in fact it was discouraged as the powers that be liked everyone to be kept in their particular box. If you did comedy you stuck with that or if you were considered a TV actor then you couldn't do film or if you wrote you shouldn't direct. So many rules set by an invisible showbiz Wizard of Oz. Best to ignore, keep Mai Zetterling's advice in mind and just crack on.

I'd had a strange fascination with the Leicestershire playwright Joe Orton since I was a kid. We grew up knowing about him in Islington because: firstly, he and his lover, Kenneth Halliwell, were sent to prison for stealing and defacing books from the Essex Road library, my unofficial place of learning; and secondly, Halliwell murdered Orton then took his own life in their flat in Noel Road, which was a five-minute walk from my primary school, my official place of learning. I'd often hover around outside their flat in the hope of seeing a ghost, as someone's mum from the school swore blind she once saw a bald man (Halliwell) peering through one of the windows.

There used to be a men's public toilet near Canonbury station

155

that I'd pass on my bike on the way to Auntie Nellie's. I'd gleaned over time that men would sometimes go inside together, so one day I crept up to the doorway to take a peek and saw two men kissing with their hands shuffling around inside each other's trousers. Blimey.

When I was a bit older, *The Naked Civil Servant* starring John Hurt, about the life of Quentin Crisp, was on the telly, plus a film called *Sunday Bloody Sunday* about a couple who shared a male lover seemed to be constantly transmitted, so it's not hard to detect where my interest in homosexual men stemmed from.

Orton's plays were the first I read and the biography of his life, *Prick Up Your Ears* by John Lahr, was my purchase after winning a 'best in term' book token at Anna Scher's. When I was working with Gary Oldman in Westcliff we'd chat about Orton as he was a fan too and once said he'd love to play him in a film, which led to a phone call from Gary a couple of years later saying, 'Hey, Kath, guess what?!'

BBC Schools made a series of 'issues of the day' films under the umbrella *Scene*. I had parts in a couple but the one that made the headlines was a great piece called *Two Of Us*, about two teenage boys falling in love. I played a tiny role as the mate of one of the boy's girlfriends (natch) but it felt brilliant to be part of – for the time – such a controversial event. Thatcher's disgraceful Clause 28 put a stop to it being shown at its allocated daytime showing and it was moved to a late-night television slot instead.

I knew some gay men once I'd started in the profession but they were mostly closeted as it was still pretty rare to find anyone who was happily 'out', and this got me thinking: *What if someone was so terrified of being 'found out' for being gay that it led to them doing something terrible?*

I had a portable typewriter bought from the money I earned working with Alex Cox and thought of two characters, George and Weaver, who I placed in a shabby attic bedsit room sometime in the late 1950s, and wrote an opening conversation. It wasn't bad so I kept writing until it turned into an actual scene.

Right, I thought, *I should keep this going until a job turns up.* Then one did.

FUN TIMES

I'd first seen Simon Brint and Rowland Rivron when they played with Mandi Symonds the night I met Rik Mayall. Since then the band had evolved into the characters Ken Bishop (keyboard, neck brace Simon) and his stepson Duane Bishop (drums, fags, booze Rowland), called themselves Raw Sex and were now supporting Dawn French and Jennifer Saunders in their live shows, which I had seen. I thought they were terrific so was really chuffed when the boys came to find me in the Old Red to ask if I'd consider joining them. They had a run at the King's Head in Islington booked along with a three-week stint at the Gilded Balloon, Edinburgh, during the festival. This time they were going to be headlining so the show needed to be longer than usual, which was why they approached me.

I had a think about what sort of character might fit in with their already dysfunctional family and came up with Tina Bishop, her back story being she hailed from Keighley, was heavily pregnant from a holiday fling with Duane so they married at Ken's insistence and she joined the act as Tina the Amazing Memory Woman who knew everything there was to know about . . . what? What could she be an expert in? To which Rowly enthusiastically suggested 'Darts!' She was also hard as nails, puffed on a ciggie and swigged from a bottle of lager without a care for her unborn child as she knew it, too, would be ''ard as fooking nails'. The boys loved it.

We worked into the show that Tina would come on after Ken and Duane did a couple of numbers, give her terrible memory act where she couldn't remember a thing because of being pregnant, leave, then come on again towards the end where she ate her pregnancy craving of a banana dipped into a cold tin of baked beans, which brought on contractions, so Ken and Duane had to carry her off the stage with her legs akimbo.

It didn't always go down well. One review in particular just said my contribution was 'not funny', but I took it on the chins and focused on the people who *loved* Tina instead, which was mostly Simon and Rowly.

It was interesting to suddenly be part of the live comedy scene. The majority of people were lovely, but some were bitter and angry about others being more successful, declaring that so-and-so had nicked their act, or so-and-so was quite simply shit. I'd get pissed and lairy and shout in some poor bugger's face that *they* were shit and also a cunt, which wasn't very cool but did put a stop to the moaning. I'd be full of regret the next day but Simon would reassure me in his gentle voice, 'Don't worry about it. We were all drunk, I doubt anyone will remember. I certainly don't.' Simon was so lovely and sweet-natured. He was hilarious as Ken, but he also composed music for television including *French and Saunders*, and he and nut-nut Rowly would soon be a regular fixture in the girls' sketch shows.

After the successful King's Head and Edinburgh runs the boys asked if I'd like to continue performing with them, as corporate gigs were starting to happen, which paid handsomely. It was a no-brainer. I loved hanging out with them, so getting paid to have such a good time was a bonus.

The shows could get pretty chaotic depending on Rowly's mischievous mood. I had to brace myself as sometimes he'd let off a firework from the stage, shouting, 'Tina! Duck, my love!' Then during one gig he had a small fire extinguisher by his bongos and I wondered what it was for as Tina was tucking into her banana and beans when *whoosh!* he set himself on fire. Most of the corporate audiences loved the anarchy and would cheer at the end for more, but some would either be nonplussed, horrified or downright angry. The latter happened at a gig at Chelsea Army Barracks. This crowd were not impressed, got fidgety and started heckling. I didn't help matters by saying into the microphone, 'Give Ireland back to the Irish!'

To which Duane said, 'Ooh, fucking hell, start the car!'

I drunkenly berated myself afterwards as we drank in a club in town. Not because I could've got the boys' heads kicked in but moaned instead that 'as I was being Tina not myself and she's a proud, white-rose woman of Yorkshire, she certainly wouldn't have the same political views as me so I was completely out of character!' The boys just looked at me as if I were mad. It was always a fun time.

Rowly, as a new character called Dr Scrote, began working on a chat show for Channel 4 called *The Last Resort*, which was presented by a young unknown named Jonathan Ross. It was broadcast live in front of a studio audience and was a great watch. As well as normal guests and music groups, the legendary Peter Cook would often appear as a variety of different characters along with a comedic artist who specialised in charcoal and silliness called Vic Reeves. Then, for some bonkers reason, Rowly suggested I should go on as Tina Bishop. I wasn't too sure about it. I relied on Simon and Rowly and didn't think I'd have the nerve to do her on my own, especially on live television, but after much encouragement from the two of them I said yes.

I was absolutely shitting myself. I phoned Tilly in a panic an hour before the show was due to air, knowing she and Ade were at home waiting to watch. 'I can't do it, Till! I can't do it! It's going to be shit!' She did her best to reassure me but, 'Why the fuck did I agree to this?! I'm fucking terrified, Till! It's fucking terrifying!'

All I remember is standing in the wings, waiting to go on in Tina's huge fake pregnancy belly, gripping a bottle of lager in a very sweaty hand, with a lit cigarette between my shaking fingers. The brilliant reggae band Aswad were just finishing a number when their drummer, Drummie Zeb, caught my eye, nodded and gave a reassuring smile and suddenly I was calm.

Tina went down well and I did another four shows I think, but the best ones were with Rowly, particularly one where we did a live link from a swimming pool. Those were the days.

Around this same time period Dawn French and Jennifer Saunders asked me to join them in a parody sketch about top pop combo Bananarama for their hugely successful TV show's Christmas special. I'd seen them live and was a big fan so was tickled pink to be asked. God, it was fun. The parody group was called Lananeeneenoonoo and we were three very shallow and very stupid girlies. Not only were Dawn and Jen brilliant and hilarious in the sketch, they were also gorgeous to hang out with, like proper showbiz big sisters. We laughed loads and I think I would've been happy if that had been my only time working with them, but the sketch would lead to us recording a single with the actual Bananarama for Comic Relief and, for me, an on-off working relationship that would last for many years to come.

Not long after this, Dawn and Jennifer were going on tour with Raw Sex as support and asked if I wanted to take part. I could be Tina with the boys then join the girls as Lananeeneenoonoo at the end of their set. It was, of course, extremely tempting and the money would've been great and much needed, but something I'd been waiting years for had finally happened, so I packed my trunk for a different adventure instead.

A GREAT PLAY

I'd had lots of auditions for theatre work, mostly modern classics or new writing, but never got the part. I'd be told constantly through Anna that they liked me *blah blah blah* but it was between myself and someone else *blah blah blah* and then the someone else was always who they wanted. *Blah*.

Until finally my luck changed. A new play called *Amongst Barbarians* was going to be on at the Royal Exchange Theatre in the heart of Manchester's city centre and I was asked to audition. I'd been to the Exchange to see Elaine in a play a couple of years earlier so it was already on my I'd-love-to-work-there wish list.

The play itself was brilliant and, much like Bob's play *Therapy*, completely ahead of its time. Its contemporary setting is Malaysia and it tells the story of two young British boys caught smuggling heroin out of the country so they are imprisoned and subsequently sentenced to death by hanging. I played Lilly, the sister of one of the boys, whose family along with the other boy's mother travel over in the hope of getting them released or at least having their sentences reduced. It was the best play I had ever read, particularly as it showed the English 'better than thou' attitude abroad, and I desperately wanted to be in it.

I could tell the director, James Maxwell, wasn't too sure about me at my first audition but luckily its writer, Michael Wall, was there for my recall and beamed at me after my reading, saying, 'Oh yes, it's got to be you.' James flashed him a look as if to say *You shouldn't have said that* but Michael just looked back at him and said, 'It *has* to be her. She's been the best.' So I got the job.

The rehearsal period was great fun. The cast were fab and I made another longtime friend in Ronan Vibert who played one of the boys. We shared digs along with Sakuntala Ramanee, who played a lawyer. Ronan and I would sit up late into the night, drinking, smoking spliffs and dissecting the play like proper wanky actors. This wasn't Sakuntala's vibe, so instead we would join her and her mum and dad as they would often visit and cook a scrumptious feast, 'Come, you must eat with us, we have lots of vegetarian dishes.' My veggie choices had also gone up a notch at the Exchange as there was a fantastic green-room canteen that would make a plate a mile high with jacket potatoes and salad or a broccoli and cheese bake or, my absolute favourite, cheese and potato pie.

I got on well with our director, James. His wife, the brilliant Avril Elgar, was playing my mum so I couldn't have slagged him off anyway, which was a good thing because it made me question certain decisions he was making respectfully to his face. He was far more experienced and learned than me, so was usually right about everything, but one time he let me have the last say.

The penultimate scene of the play has the two families together in a hotel room, getting more and more drunk as they've been told there is no longer any hope for the boys so they will be hanged the following day. It's a brilliant and terrifying scene, full of pain and chaos. My character, who is also off her head, enters, puts on the radio and turns it up loud. I can't remember the name of the song James wanted to be playing but it was very mawkish and felt too on the nose. I thought it should be a jolly pop song, 'I think the song choice is wrong, James, it should feel odd and add to the mess that's going on, not underscore it with sympathy.'

'Oh!' he said to the room with kind amusement, 'this one is trying to direct the play! What do *you* suggest it should be?'

I thought for a moment then, 'How about "I Should Be So Lucky" by Kylie Minogue?'

When we came to the scene during the technical rehearsals the mawkish song was played through the stage speaker and I just thought, *Oh well, he didn't like my idea.* We had a tea break then went through the scene again, but this time when my character Lilly flicked on the radio, Kylie's voice came out instead. I was happy James was giving it a chance but didn't expect him to use it for the show. However, when we gathered for the note session at the end of the day he finished by saying, 'I'm feeling that Miss Burke is right. "I Should Be So Lucky" *will* be playing on the radio. It adds to the horror we're witnessing. Thank you, Kathy.' I was over the fucking moon and full of pride that the song got mentioned in some of the reviews, even though it was a tiny moment.

The play itself was a huge success, playing to full houses, and we partied hard in Manchester with the stage crew after the performances, dancing in The Haçienda or drinking in the Press Club till the sun came up.

The play then got another run at the Hampstead Theatre in London. This tiny but prolific and respected space was also packed for every show, with the added bonus that being in London meant family and friends could see it along with directors, producers and the like so hopefully it would lead to more work in the future. It also turned up an unexpected and lovely surprise: Pat and Meir from my childhood. They'd seen my name in a review, so came along to watch. It was great to see them, and I was chuffed at how proud they were of me.

Oh, and I had to pop back up north to pick up a Manchester Evening News Theatre Award for my performance, which was the cherry on top of an already delicious cake.

It was a remarkable play. A standout moment for me that I've talked about many times over the years was when the boys are being prepared for their deaths. Ronan's character, Ralph, who has been stoic throughout, suddenly crumbles as his hands are tied behind his back, 'I can't free my hands. I will never see my beautiful hands again.'

I still think about this line today, usually when I'm doing a frustrating mundane task like trying to get a jar open. I'll stop for a moment, take a breath and appreciate the miracle of my hands.

A MUSE

I was reaching my quarter of a century and life at home had changed once again. John had finally moved into his own flat, which was only up the road and round a corner. He was working as a teacher of graphic design at Epsom School of Art and had a very lovely girlfriend called Jane. Let's just take a moment and give this young man a round of applause. It was now just me and Dad rattling around in the big house.

Dad had gone without the drink for quite a while and was working as a swimming pool caretaker, which he liked even more than the park keeping, but now it was me that was coming home at all hours, if at all, drunk and sometimes raging. He'd get upset and worried about me, but I didn't care and would be cunty, saying things like, 'You can fucking talk!' or my favourite, 'This is karma!' Poor bloke. I think his years of cheap whisky intake had wiped his own misdemeanours from his memory because he'd look at me with a sad puzzlement as I slammed doors and smashed plates in the kitchen on purpose.

Nothing much seemed to happen after *Amongst Barbarians* finished its run at Hampstead. I went back to doing the odd small role but also started to turn jobs down if I felt they were clichéd or just badly written. Not every middle-class writer knew how a working-class person spoke, and sometimes the parts could be downright offensive, so I thought best not to be involved in the first place despite missing out on the money.

I went back to writing my play, which was very nearly finished. I had Bob Pugh in mind as I was writing the Weaver character, and Perry Fenwick was who I'd originally been thinking of for

George, but I'd met someone in Manchester who struck me as better suited.

I'd spotted James Clyde in the green-room canteen at the Exchange and liked his look. Perry was fit and tanned from playing football, but Jim was long-limbed, scrawny and pale with jet-black hair. He was good-looking but not overly handsome and reminded me of actors from the 1950s I'd seen in black and white movies on the telly. He looked more George to me and I'd now made the character needy for alcohol so his pallor especially fitted.

I went over, introduced myself, asked if he was a Buddhist as his clothes suggested he might be. He said no, then I asked if he was an actor, to which he said yes. He was in rehearsals for *A Taste of Honey* that was on at the Exchange after *Amongst Barbarians*. I went to see it and thought he was great so continued with him in mind when I went back to the typewriter and apologised to Perry.

Things had also changed at the Old Red. Glaswegian-born 'Whispering' Ken McClymont from the Scottish contingent had taken over as artistic director of the theatre under my encouragement. We'd become close friends before I'd headed to Manchester and I really liked his taste and ideas for the theatre. It was a tough job to take on. The money was of course crap but he also had to contend with Tony and Pauline being his bosses, as they had their own rules about the place, including no play could run longer than two and a half hours or they wouldn't get the takings behind the bar, and no plays about the IRA, as there had been one on years before that led to a big old fisticuffs.

Ken settled in quickly, having worked in theatre many times

during some of Edinburgh's festivals. He was a fine artist by trade but that was pretty isolating and he liked 'the mad heads of the theatre folk'. As I was often without work, Ken asked if I wanted to help with reading plays for him. His office was a few doors along from the pub, up some very rickety stairs that led to the top floor and into a very dusty room piled high with unsolicited scripts. No wonder he needed help. How on earth could he get through them all?

'You usually know by page ten if a play is any good,' he said. 'If the dialogue is crap or characters don't ring true or it just isn't grabbing your attention, put it on the reject pile and move on to the next.'

This seemed quite mercenary to me. All that hard work and effort and we just dismissed them within a few pages? *Nah*, I thought, *that's not very respectful* and was determined to plough on regardless, but after a while of doing what I thought was only fair I had to hold my hands up and agree with him, 'Fuck me, Ken, most of these are rubbish!'

'Aye, hen, just up to page ten, remember?'

It was great fun hanging out with him. We'd laugh all the time and go to see as many plays as we could afford, but the reading of other new plays really helped with the writing of my own.

Along with the aforementioned George (mid-twenties, shy, people pleaser) and Weaver (thirties, coarse, brutish), my play now had the added characters Gordon (forty, ex-military, posh), Mrs Tebbit (forty, sex-starved, landlady) and Mr Thomas (forty, gentle, missing tenant of the house). I decided to call it *Mr Thomas*, as the first half consisted of conversations as to where he could possibly be.

I was incredibly nervous about showing it to anyone. I couldn't afford to put it on anyway as I'd worked out I would need at least five grand, which made my bank balance laugh in my over-ambitious face. I shied away for ages until Ken got fed up hearing me talk about it and snapped, 'Will you just let me read the bloody thing!'

So I did, and he loved it.

THE PLAY READING

Play readings in front of an invited audience were and still are a common occurrence if you want to get a sense of how people will react or if you need to drum up some funds, and I was after both.

I sent the play to James Clyde, who was very much on board, and was just waiting for Bob Pugh to get back to me. Ken really loved *Mr Thomas* and was very excited about the prospect of it being on at the Old Red, more so than me even because he didn't have the added stress of nerves. We sorted out an afternoon that the reading could take place and sent the play out to some other actors that would be willing to do it as there wouldn't be a fee for the reading, just expenses. I'd done a few readings for free myself over the years so didn't feel funny about it.

Then something happened that I hadn't been expecting at all. Bob didn't like it and didn't want to do it. What?! I was absolutely gobsmacked *and* devastated. I'd written the bloody thing with him in mind and now I was in a spin. My confidence was shattered. Bob was who I looked up to and whose opinion mattered to me more than most.

I met Ken for a drink in the pub. He was really confused, 'I'm shocked, hen. Weaver is a fantastic character so I'm very surprised Bob isn't up for it.'

I was despondent. 'It's shit, Ken. It must be shit if he doesn't like it.'

Ken tried to reassure me. 'Look, I think it's great, James Clyde thinks it's great and you just need to carry on and think of somebody else for Weaver.'

We sat for a while trying to think of who else we could

approach but absolutely nobody was coming to mind. Bob had been so clear in my head while writing, he just wouldn't leave.

The Old Red's main entrance was on St John Street but it also had a back door you could come in through from an alleyway on Goswell Road, directly opposite the old entrance to Angel Tube station. We always sat at the table nearest to the back door as it was where the pool table was and the closest to the theatre entrance. I'd noticed earlier that there were some film trucks nearby but thought no more about it.

Ken and I were huddled over an old *Spotlight* book, looking for inspiration, when the back door flew open and in walked a flustered actor wearing a shabby period costume, with scruffy hair and a sweaty complexion. It was Ray Winstone. We both followed him with our eyes, watched as he ordered then drank down a pint of lager in one then asked for another. Ken and I looked at each other without saying a word, but our eyes were now wide and twinkling.

'Isn't he too young, though?' I said to Ken under my breath.

'He's younger than Bob, aye, but I don't think that matters really. Does it?'

I thought about it for a moment while I stared at Ray, imagining him in the role. I'd met him in the pub a couple of years earlier. It had actually been Perry who introduced us. We'd played a game of pool, which I won so he said I must be a lesbian. He certainly wasn't a regular, and the chances of seeing him in there again were very slim, so I knew I had to grab this rare opportunity.

'Hello, Ray. I'm Kathy, we had a game of pool one time, I'm Perry's mate.'

'Oh, hello babe,' he said, completely uninterested.

'I'm doing a play reading in a couple of weeks and there's a part I'd love you to look at if you'd be up for it?'

'Nah,' he said, 'I don't do theatre, there's no money in it.'

My heart sank again but I pushed on. 'It's only a reading so not a proper commitment.'

But again he said no, adding a thanks for asking then turned back to his pint.

I went back to the table but Ken wasn't there. I sat with my drink and carried on flicking through *Spotlight* when Ken came back in, a bit flustered. He'd run to the office to get a copy of the script but I told him Ray had said no.

'Just give it another go,' Ken said, 'what's the worst that can happen?'

So I went over again, script in hand. 'Hi Ray, sorry, I know you said you're not interested, but if you could just read it I'd love to know what you think about it, even if you don't want to do it. My number's on there so just give us a ring when you've read it and let me know.'

He begrudgingly said okay, put the now rolled-up script into his pocket, downed the rest of his drink and left. I honestly didn't think I'd hear from him again, so was more than pleasantly surprised when he rang the following day.

'Did you write that?'

Yes, I said.

'All on your own?'

Again, I said yes.

'You write how people talk. Is my character an iron?' Iron hoof is cockney rhyming and queer slang for poof.

'Er, yes,' I said, 'but he's obviously confused and terrified about being found out, especially during the period it's set in.'

'Yea,' he said, 'he would be. So is he in love with George, then?'

Again, I said yes, but he doesn't know how to handle it.

'Mmm, he's fucked in the head with it all, ain't he?'

Yes, I said, he is. I was holding my breath while he paused.

'Yea, alright, I'll do the reading.'

We had a small rehearsal the day before the reading and Ray was amazing. He was perfect for the role, like I'd written with him in mind from the off.

Everyone myself and Ken invited to the reading showed up, including people we knew with money. I'd also invited Phil Davis as I wanted him to direct. I can't remember why I didn't want to direct it myself, that was what I eventually wanted to do after all, but I think I might've felt it would be pushing things a bit and could put a potential producer off. Female theatre directors were still a rarity, especially one with no experience, so I guess I didn't want to shoot myself in the foot. Besides, I was still really enjoying being an actor and I'd also written the play in the hope of getting better or at least more interesting parts. If they could see I had a brain in my head maybe it would shift a stereotype mindset?

The first half of the reading went down very well, with the audience laughing in all the right places. I had a quick drink with Ken at the interval while he made reassuring noises, then back up to the theatre for the second half – which also went well, with a generous round of applause, whoops and cheers after the stage direction 'Blackout'.

Down in the bar afterwards, people were chatting noisily and Tilly and Elaine were buzzing, telling me it *worked* and I should feel proud, and Perry was extremely gracious saying he thought

James was perfect. I was preoccupied with thoughts of how many people might contribute towards it. I had two grand put aside myself, again the teeth fixing was put on the back burner, but still needed another three grand, and if fifteen or so people put in a couple of hundred quid maybe we'd reach a doable target.

Phil Davis came over to me and Ken. 'It's very good but I'm not going to direct it because I think you should direct it yourself.'

Oh. I wasn't expecting him to say that.

Then lovely Simon Brint from Raw Sex joined us. 'May I ask what's being discussed?'

I told him that Phil thought I should direct it myself, to which he said, 'Oh yes, I totally agree. How much do you need to put it on?'

So I told him five grand but I'd only need three as I could put two in myself and . . . but he stopped my chatter and said, 'I'll give you the whole five thousand but you absolutely have to direct it yourself otherwise no deal.'

I couldn't believe it.

Ken went off to a table with Simon to discuss all the financial doings, how much money would be needed for rehearsals, how much for the set, etc., and I think I just sat with Perry and the girls, getting steadily and happily pissed till closing time.

IN THE MEANTIME

Ken had booked a slot for *Mr Thomas* to be on at the Old Red the following year but in the meantime I had to get on with working as an actor.

The exact order of things is a bit fuzzy in my old brain but I headed off to Ibiza at some point to be in a film for *The Comic Strip Presents* . . . called *Funseekers*. Written by playwright Doug Lucie and *Comic Strip* regular Nigel Planer, it tells the story of a group of people on an 18–30 holiday jaunt. That's all I can remember. I have no recollection about who my character was or how long I was there but it must've been a couple of weeks. This was pre-Ibiza mania time so the place itself was pretty quiet, which is hard to imagine now.

Katrin Cartlidge and Michèle Winstanley were also in it so once again it was nice to have pals around. It was fun but I was pretty drunk most evenings. One night I stupidly let an equally drunk as me crew member give me a piggyback as I was exhausted from bucking a bronco for over an hour, but he tripped and I went over his head and landed full face on to the concrete pavement. Katrin kindly stayed with me in my room till the morning as she was worried I might have concussion. I was okay but the make-up lady was very pissed off.

Around this time, Jonathan Ross had a new show on Sunday nights called *One Hour with Jonathan Ross*. Included was a game show, 'Knock Down Ginger', which involved comedy characters behind doors asking the questions for the contestants who were members of the public. I was asked to take part as Tina Bishop and the other performers were Vic Reeves, his new partner in crime Bob Mortimer and two blokes I hadn't met before, Charlie Higson and Paul Whitehouse. It was nice to dust off Tina's costume but the job itself wasn't very satisfying. Like *The Last Resort* it was broadcast live and in front of a studio audience, but our contributions felt very quick. As far as I can remember we had weekly contracts as the producers didn't know if the game would be included in every episode. We'd turn up late morning, talk about new characters if needed, do a tech, then the show itself. I felt Tina was being wasted. She had much more airtime on *The Last Resort* so it felt like I was taking a step backwards. Paul Whitehouse agreed with me, saying, 'You should come up with another character.' Then suggested, 'I think you'd be great at playing a little boy.' *Oh*, I thought, *that's a good idea*.

I went down into the studio's costume store and cobbled together a school uniform of sorts. I then joined Paul and the others.

'Okay, I've been thinking, what if he's actually a pubescent teenager rather than a little boy, then I can make him quite surly?'

'What does he sound like?' asked Paul.

I mumbled a bit, then had a eureka moment. 'He's going through puberty so what if his voice is constantly breaking?'

I tried it and Paul laughed his head off. 'That's great!'

Now all I had to do was think of a name. We were a couple of hours from going on air and, being a conscientious soul, I thought I'd better warn and check something with a friend so I made a quick phone call from my dressing room.

'Hi mate, just a quick one, I'm doing a new character on the show tonight and want to name him after you. Is that okay? It's a really fast bit and I might only do him this once so hopefully it won't get on your nerves or anything.'

My friend said it was cool, no problem and was actually quite flattered.

I went back to Paul and the lads. 'Got it. He's going to be called Perry, Perry the pubescent teenager. My mate Perry Fenwick says it's okay.'

On the show itself, before our game-show slot, a guest had been on with Jonathan, causing a bit of a stir. I can't remember the exact details, but it involved him handcuffing our host to a chair and making a big old twit of himself. This was great for me because when I was revealed as Perry I improvised in his high-pitch, low-pitch voice, 'Hello, I'm Perry the pubescent teenager and like that bloke earlier, I'm still waiting for my balls to drop.' Big laughs.

Later in the bar I somehow discovered that the boys were getting more money than me. What? That couldn't be right. We were all doing the same amount of work. I was already peeved that the money wasn't as good as what I earned on *The Last Resort* but understood once I knew there would be more of us performing. However, I didn't expect to be on less because I was a woman, otherwise I wouldn't have done the job in the first place. What to do?

When it came to the cheerios, Paul said, 'I'll see you next week.'

And I said, 'No you won't.'

It was a small act of defiance, some may say stupidity, because let's face it, I wasn't exactly of any real importance to the show or showbiz in general. But I just couldn't continue with it feeling the way I did, which was ripped off, because I was and in general women were.

JUMP AROUND

The rave scene was giving it large, but I wasn't very interested. I'd first been aware of MDMA when I was doing *Straight to Hell*. A particular person was very touchy-feely with me in the hotel bar one night, which was a bit disconcerting until James Fearnley explained, 'Don't worry, she's on Ecstasy, it'll wear off soon.' By the late '80s it had reached a wider consumer beyond the rock and roll community and everyone seemed to be on it. Except me. I'd already been refusing cocaine whenever it was offered as I didn't like the way people behaved under its influence. I was cocky enough already so needed no help in that department.

The downsides of not taking it were I was always more drunk than everyone else, without a 'quick straightener', and there were longer waiting times for the ladies' loos. This would give me the hump if I had a bladder full of lager and I'd bang on cubicle doors, shouting, 'Can you be quicker getting that gear up your nose, please! Some of us actually have to use the fucking toilet!' Ecstasy was just another chemical as far as I was concerned and although I quite liked people when they were 'on it', being in their company during the comedowns wasn't as pleasant, so I decided again that it wasn't for me.

The booze was still my friend but was becoming not as much fun. I was getting pissed quicker and getting into dodgy situations, like waking up with blokes I didn't know or couldn't remember meeting, or leaving the pub without saying goodbye and causing worry for my mates, or falling asleep in the pub itself and having to be shaken awake by Tony, 'Come on, you, we've ordered you a cab.'

I knew the booze was making me miserable but knocking it on the head hadn't even crossed my mind. I was still great fun the majority of times and, to be honest, I didn't know how to stop or who I would be without it. I'd drunk most nights since I was sixteen and on the rare occasions I didn't drink the sleep deprivation would make me unfocused at work so that was the best excuse to carry on.

Dad was still booze-free and had started to take himself off on holidays around Europe. I loved having the house to myself and would bring home all sorts to party but nobody took the piss too much, so Dad was unaware when he returned home.

The best times I had were seeing The Pogues. Everyone was pissed at their gigs so I fitted in rather nicely. The first time I went to see them wasn't that long after *Straight to Hell*, at the since-shutdown Kilburn National with Tilly. The place was already packed by the time we weaved our way to the bar, and I felt a little nervous, 'I think we should just stay here, Till, it feels like it's going to get a bit rowdy.' Tilly nodded in agreement.

The band came on, the music kicked in and the crowd went wild. The next thing I knew I'd turned to Tilly, shouted in her ear that I'd see her in a bit and made my way to the front of the throng and jumped around like a teenager for the duration of the gig. It was brilliant. The band were brilliant. They were so much better than any bands I'd seen as a kid. It was exhilarating. I found James particularly impressive as he leaped about the stage with his extremely heavy accordion. *Blimey*, I thought, *no wonder he goes for an hour swim every morning.*

I went to many more of their gigs, including all four nights at the Town and Country Club in Kentish Town. Their massive worldwide hit 'Fairytale of New York' had been released the

Christmas before so the beautiful Kirsty MacColl would join them for that number. She was a great and very funny person.

Everyone who was anyone wanted to see the band live, and I got to say hello to lots of cool cats including Ronnie Drew from The Dubliners and Christy Moore, but was rendered speechless when David Bowie rocked up.

I saw them play again a couple of years later, in 1991, and Ronan came with me. It was at Glasgow's famous Barrowland Ballroom. It was St Patrick's Day and Celtic had slaughtered Rangers in a footy match earlier in the day. Not only was it the best I'd ever seen them play, it was also the most electric, most sweaty and most joyous night out I'd had in my life so far. It couldn't be topped – so I didn't bother trying and never saw them play live again.

DIRECTOR/ACTOR

James Clyde's partner, Deirdre Strath, a quiet, redheaded beauty of Irish descent, was born and raised in New York. She and Jim had been together since their first day at RADA and are still together today, with the addition of their daughter, Ruby.

They invited me to their flat off the Holloway Road for some dinner and a proposition. They had cobbled together some money to be in a two-handed, one-act play by American writer Lanford Wilson, called *Home Free!*, and asked if I'd like to direct. The production was to be on at a small fringe theatre in Earl's Court called The Finborough and would have just a couple of weeks' rehearsal. I wasn't too sure. My only experience of directing had been in assisting Bob on *Therapy* and directing a play reading of an adaptation of Émile Zola's *Thérèse Raquin*. Since then I had only really thought about directing *Mr Thomas* when the time came.

Deirdre felt it would be good practice for me before *Mr T* and really wanted me to do it. I'd seen her act in another play some months before and thought she was great, and I was already a fan of Jim of course, so I took a copy of the play home to give it a read.

Home Free! is a surreal piece about a brother and sister in an implied incestuous relationship. The dialogue was brilliant and sharp and I could envisage Jim and Deirdre in the roles. I wasn't crazy about it, to be honest, as I found it a bit too 'out there' but took on board what D said about it being good practice, so I said yes and thank you very much for the trust.

Its two-week run at The Finborough had been booked in advance, and at the time I agreed to do it no other work was happening but then something came along I couldn't possibly turn down.

The BBC had decided to do a televised version of *Amongst Barbarians* that would be directed by Jane Howell who I'd worked with before, doing a small role in something I can't remember. I went along for what I was told would be a meeting not an audition as she'd seen me play Lilly at Hampstead and wanted me to play her again.

Jane was a formidable, chain-smoking woman. Back then you could smoke pretty much anywhere, including BBC meeting rooms, and she made me look like an amateur. She told me that myself and Ricardo Sibelo who had played the barman were the only two actors from the original production that she wanted for her version. I was stunned. What about Ronan and Avril Elgar, who had both been phenomenal? Nope, she had her own ideas for casting and hoped I would still come on board.

I was torn. I absolutely wanted to do it but Ronan and I had become really great friends who saw each other all the time as he and his then girlfriend, Emma, had also become Old Red Lion regulars. We met for a drink. Ronan was gutted as he'd already heard from his agent that it wasn't going to go his way, but was adamant that we have a good night and celebrate the fact it had at least worked out for me. It was good of him to be so understanding, as I doubt I would've reacted as generously if the shoe was on the other foot.

There was now just the problem of telling Jim and Deirdre, but they quickly came up with a solution, 'You'll still be free for the rehearsals, and our friend Rufus Norris said he's happy to do the technical and open the show.' Oh. Okay then. And so began my first job as a theatre director.

We had very enjoyable and stress-free rehearsals. Jim and Deirdre worked incredibly well together without any upset, which I remember being very impressed with especially as they were in a relationship and living together. Rufus came to see a run once I'd blocked it out, then took over while I went off to do *Amongst Barbarians*.

The new cast for *Amongst Barbarians* included Lee Ross and Con O'Neill as the condemned men and David Jason as the dad of Lee's character, Bryan, and my character, Lilly.

I enjoyed it. Lilly was the best part I'd had so far and it felt really good having the opportunity to play her again, especially for television. Jane was a wonderful director, the whole cast were dynamite in their roles and good fun to be around, but it was a very bittersweet experience, and out of respect for Ronan I didn't do my usual invite to the Old Red once we'd finished recording.

I managed to see one performance of *Home Free!*, which was great, but looking back I regret directing Jim to have his back to the audience for his character's opening speech. Maybe I was trying to be 'out there' with my direction, but I think it was actually a bit wanky of me and not a choice I would make now.

Rufus had done some exceptional work with the lighting and sound, which made me feel a bit weird about taking full credit as its director. He didn't mind and twenty or so years later he became the artistic director of the National Theatre in London, so being uncredited didn't do him much harm in the long run. And Deirdre recently reminded me that a young Alison Goldfrapp designed the poster for us – 'Ooh La La'!

A SHOWBIZ ANECDOTE

I don't tell this story much as it's very showy-offy but, fuck it, isn't that what a memoir's for?

The Secret Policeman's Ball had been running for a few years, doing music and comedy concerts to raise funds for the charity Amnesty International. Jennifer Saunders was getting together the 'biggest ball' along with John Cleese and she asked if I would do a spot as Tina Bishop. I didn't want to do her on my own as I'd be a tiny tadpole in a massive pool of extremely funny fish including Peter Cook, Dudley Moore, Michael Palin, Lenny Henry and Jennifer herself along with Dawn. I asked Simon Brint if he would be Ken Bishop and accompany me on the keyboard while Tina gave an out-of-tune rendition of the song 'The Way We Were' as she mistakenly thought the show was raising funds for Amnesia International.

We did three consecutive nights and, once again, Tina divided the crowd. It was nerve-wracking but pretty incredible to be among such established comedy stars, and on the final show when I went back to my dressing room Peter Cook was sitting on the floor, a little worse for wear.

'Oh, hello,' I said shyly. 'I think you might be in the wrong room.'

'I'm not,' he said. 'I've been waiting for you because I wanted to tell you I think you're a fucking genius.'

I didn't know how to react, so laughed nervously and said, 'That's a bit over the top.'

He got himself up, lit a cigarette, turned before leaving the room, and said, 'No it fucking isn't. If I say you're a genius then you bloody well *are* one – and never fucking forget it!'

So I haven't.

MR THOMAS

It wasn't going to be easy. Jim and Ray were very much committed, and a lovely Yorkshire-born actor called Ian Jentle was on board to play Mr Thomas, and James Snell was going to be Gordon. Mrs Tebbit, the sex-starved landlady, was more tricky to find. Linda Marlowe, who was known for her great work with Steven Berkoff, had done the reading but wasn't available for the actual production. There was no way I was going to do the part myself as I was still only twenty-five and she was in her forties and I certainly didn't want the extra pressure, or for it to become a full-blown vanity project. Ken and I were back scanning through *Spotlight* but the actresses I sent the play out to were either unavailable or couldn't afford to do a box-office split or simply didn't like it.

I was becoming edgy. We were approaching Christmas and rehearsals were starting the first working week of January. I phoned Tilly, my go-to in a panic, 'It's a nightmare, Till! Nobody wants to do it. It's all going to shit, Till! It's all going to shit!!' She calmed me and said she'd have a think. An hour or so later she rang me back and told me about a woman she'd worked with on a quick job earlier in the year, 'She's called Anita Graham, she was very nice and very attractive but was certainly around forty. I don't know what she's done before but she was very good on the job.'

Ken had a chat with her agent, then Anita gave me a call and the next day popped round to my house to pick up the script. I liked her immediately. She was much more glamorous-looking than I wanted Mrs Tebbit to be but she assured me that without make-up, or with the wrong make-up, 'I can look like an old boot'. She took the script, rang me before the day ended and said she loved it. *Phew.*

A young designer, Matthew Duguid, was on board to make the set. I wanted it to be as realistic as possible: a room within a room, with a sink, wardrobe, floor lamp, armchair, all dominated by a rickety double bed. Its palette was greens and browns, set off with touches of damp. Matt did a fantastic job and along with John Pope's lighting design it was the best set I'd ever seen at the Old Red.

I asked my brother John if he could design the poster and leaflets for us. I wanted the image to be a photo of Mr Thomas with his back to camera and touching his ear, which was a signal the homosexual community used in the '50s to let each other know they were that way inclined, bearing in mind that it was still illegal back then. John took a photo of Ian then did the graphics around him with the play's information including 'A KEN BISHOP PRODUCTION' in honour of Simon. It was perfect and very classy.

Actor and friend Wayne 'Pickles' Norman was starting to do a bit of stage management here and there, as he too was getting bored with waiting around for acting jobs. I asked if he'd be up for working on *Mr Thomas* as its deputy stage manager, which meant running the show from the sound and lighting board, and luckily for me he was.

Rehearsals started well, but before the second week was done, James Snell (Gordon) informed me that a play he'd just been in now had a West End transfer so he was terribly sorry but would have to leave. *What?!* He had a friend lined up to take over so I wasn't to worry. *What?!* His name is Oliver Smith, he was in the movie *Hellraiser* (which I hadn't seen) and he's more than happy to step into the breach. Flipping heck. I didn't have much choice so said farewell to James and hello, welcome and thank you to Oliver.

They were a proper mixed bunch. Ian was a communist and called everyone comrade or brother, which drove Ray up the wall. He came up to me at the beginning of week three, saying there might be a problem, comrade. *What the fuck now?*

'I've an uncle who is knocking on death's door. I hate the old bugger but I'm his only relative so if he pegs it I'll have to head up north to sort the funeral.'

My heart sank. What the heck was I supposed to do if *that* happened?! Anita had overheard the chat, 'Sorry to interrupt, is your uncle with the Co-op, Ian?'

Ian said yes actually, he was.

'They can keep them on ice for up to six weeks, I think.'

'Oh,' said Ian. 'Do you know what, my love? I think you might be right.' Then turned back to me, saying, 'Problem solved, comrade, think no more of it.'

We moved into the theatre and the tech went smoothly. I was using a Pogues track called 'Gridlock' to open the play and it sounded great. We did a dress run, all good, then just one preview before its press night.

The preview started well enough. Jim and Ray were bouncing off each other nicely and the audience were reacting positively. Then Oliver was supposed to come on as Gordon but nothing happened. Where the fuck was he? After what felt like an age, on he finally came. He said his first couple of lines – but then nothing – and I watched horrified as the blood drained from his face. He turned to us, the audience, and said in his rather lovely, soft, posh voice, 'I'm terribly sorry, ladies and gentlemen, but I seemed to have dried. I need to go and get the book.' And then he exited to the one shared dressing room backstage. Jim as George was sitting in the armchair, quietly rolling a cigarette, but his thin body became so tense I thought he was going to snap. Ray, as Weaver, was meant to be asleep on the bed so started to do some sleepy scratches and grunts in the hope of keeping us entertained. There was a small kerfuffle from offstage then eventually, after what felt like half a fucking century, Oliver came back on with the script in his hands.

At the interval I went to the dressing room to find out what had happened. Oliver looked very sheepish, 'You told me not to have a drink before the show, my darling, and I'm afraid it might've disorientated me.' What the fuck? He was right, I had asked all of them not to drink as there was already rather a lot of it going on and I wanted them to wait till *after* the show was finished. I didn't think it was a big ask, seeing as it was a *professional* fucking job, but what I didn't know was Oliver *needed* a bloody drink, otherwise he was wracked with nerves. Ken popped to the bar and got him half a Guinness, and Anita took me to one side.

'I couldn't believe it when he came back into the dressing room. I said, what you back here for? And he said he couldn't do it and he wasn't going back on, and I said you bloody well are, mate, I'm not having you ruin this for me! And I gave him the script and shoved him on by his arse with my foot!'

What a woman.

The second half was good and Oliver got through it without the script. I was absolutely shitting myself the following night when the press and lots of pals were in, but when I went backstage to wish the gang luck, Oliver was very happy with his medicinal Guinness and said he felt fine.

It went okay. More than okay. Ken read the reviews and although they weren't mind-blowing there were a couple of good enough ones to pique a theatregoer's interest, which led to tickets slowly being booked. One review I liked said, 'Miss Burke's use of language would shock a docker.'

It had a usual four-week run, and I was only concerned that we sold enough seats for the actors to get paid. The Friday and Saturday night shows were always the busiest at the Old Red, so no worries there, but I'd been in plays myself that could have fewer than ten people in the audience midweek, and so I had everything crossed that we'd fare a bit better than that.

We weren't on on Mondays so I turned up on the Tuesday after the opening week, expecting a small but hopefully healthy turnout. It was nearly full. Along with the reviews, word of mouth had done its job and people wanted to see it. Landlord Tony was chuffed, 'It's very nice to have a busy bar on a Tuesday, Kathleen!'

By the following Tuesday, with a full two weeks of the run left to go, Ken was waiting in the pub for me at the table closest to its main entrance. He jumped up beaming when he saw me.

'It's sold out, hen.'

Well, I was delighted. 'What, on a Tuesday? That's amazing, babe!'

'No,' he said, 'I mean the run. The whole run is sold out.'

Now I know the Old Red was tiny, with its fifty or so seats, but like any fringe theatre it was still pretty unusual for every seat to be booked for all of its remaining shows. I was elated and felt like we'd packed out the Albert Hall.

Our producer Simon was more than happy. John, Barry and Carm really liked it, and Dad was especially impressed by the, according to him, accurate portrayal of the period, constantly asking with a proud frown, 'How did you know it was like that? I knew blokes like that Weaver character on the building sites but how did *you* know?'

I just shrugged and said I dunno, from films probably.

Bob Pugh came with his partner, Maggie. I was sitting next to them and when the lights came up for the curtain call she turned to him and said, 'You stupid little prick.' And Bob nodded in regretful agreement.

In its last week director Les Blair, who I'd worked with years before, came up to me after seeing it, said he loved it and had I thought about doing a TV or film version? I hadn't and didn't think I'd want to. To me, because I'd written it with the Old Red space in mind it felt odd to think of it beyond there, but then a different, more interesting offer came our way.

A producer called Michael Custance, along with Channel 4's then-commissioning editor for arts, Waldemar Januszczak, asked to meet myself, Ken and Simon. They were going to make a series called *Small Stages*; the idea being to take five plays from the fringe and reproduce everything exactly as it was – direction, cast, set, etc. – but in a multi-camera studio with an established studio director at the helm to do all the technical stuff. They wondered if I'd be up for *Mr Thomas* being one of the five plays? This was incredible. Of course I was up for it! It couldn't be more perfect.

They sorted out the rights with Simon and it felt extremely satisfying that he would get back the five grand he'd originally invested plus a bit more on top, and everyone else involved would be paid too.

It was a brilliant way to end the run, knowing we'd all be together again later in the year for the recording. We had a big party on the last night, but I of course got very, very drunk so remember nothing about it.

WHY I LOVED DIRECTING

People would sometimes ask me if I liked directing because I liked having control. I used to think this was a bad thing, thinking it meant I was a controlling person, but now I'm older I realise of course it's about *taking* control and, more importantly for me, taking responsibility.

Because I'd written *Mr Thomas* it was fantastic to tell the story exactly as I'd envisioned it. I was able to dictate how the set and costumes should look along with choosing the right music, sound and lighting. My hands were tied somewhat with the casting side of things, because on the fringe there was no wage just the risky box-office split, but I was very happy with them all despite Oliver's original wobbles.

It was incredibly rewarding during rehearsals if an actor got stuck with a particular line or thought process and I was able to help them, and I really enjoyed blocking the play out. This part felt like choreographing a dance, making sure everyone was in their right place, as smoothly as possible, so the focus for the audience was clear and precise. Later in life this was always much easier on a bigger stage, but I still liked the smallness of the Old Red as its confinement made it feel like you were watching television.

I didn't have any particular method to my directing, that would come later, but as an actor I knew how I didn't like *being* directed, so would avoid those ways and just stuck with what I'd learned from the directors I liked, along with my own instincts.

The added bonus of being the director was not having lunch with the actors, as it was good for them to have time away from me, especially as I was also the writer. Actors need to chew the fat on their own, to discuss things they may not be happy with – or to just slag me off if they need to. Plus, it was great not having to be there for every performance once the play was up and running. I could turn up when I fancied, buy them all a drink and wallow in the praise from the audience.

It was nerve-wracking, testing and at times frustrating, but ultimately incredibly rewarding and I really hoped to do more directing in the future.

MR HATTON

Before recording *Mr Thomas* I had a couple of acting theatre jobs lined up. The first was a play called *Crux*, written by April De Angelis, directed by Saffron Myers and produced by a wonderful touring company called Paines Plough, who have recently celebrated their fiftieth anniversary. The play is set in thirteenth-century France and is about a group of women pushing back against a corrupt Pope – it was dark, bonkers and so much fun.

The cast included my old friend Steve Sweeney and an actress I'd admired for years called Anna Keaveney. A pocket rocket born in Runcorn, Annie, as she liked to be called, was already known for her brilliant portrayal of the characters Marie Jackson in Channel 4's flagship soap *Brookside*, and Jeanette, a gossipy chatterbox in the smash-hit film version of Willy Russell's play *Shirley Valentine*. I loved her. She was very funny, extremely smart and a joy to act with.

My character was the innocent of the piece, who had lovely lines like, 'This is my bucket, I forgot to let go of the handle when I left so it came with me.' And my favourite scenes were with Annie's character, who had equally memorable lines such as, 'Truth? If you want to know what truth is stick your head in a bag because it's that dark.'

We toured around Cornwall and Devon, which was very nice, and its last two weeks were at the Lyric Theatre in Hammersmith. I recently met up with its company manager Paul Crewes, who is now CEO of the Theatre Royal in York, and he jogged my memory about us doing a couple of nights in St Austell, where we had ten people in the audience for show one who informed us afterwards that they hadn't enjoyed the play but the same ten people came back the following night purely to support the theatre not us. He also reminded me that when we were in Hammersmith we'd jump in the van after the Friday night shows and head to Islington and the Old Red before the doors were shut for the lock-in, which of course didn't surprise me.

I'd been thinking about getting a new agent. I was still being represented by Anna Scher and, although I loved her very much, I hadn't been attending the classes for years, and she was still prominently known as a children's and young adults' agent. Tilly and Elaine had long since left and as I was now twenty-six, it was very much time to move on. The only problem being *Who do I go with?* I was lucky in that I'd already had letters from a few saying they'd like me to consider joining them, but after meeting them I never felt a viable connection. I didn't want to just act and I liked making my own decisions, so whoever it was had to put up with me having a mind of my own (hello).

I'd noticed Annie's agent, Stephen Hatton, was the only agent of the *Crux* cast who bothered travelling the long distance from London to Cornwall to see her in the play and also came more than once to its Hammersmith run, bringing casting directors and producers along with him. I asked Annie if she thought it was worth me approaching him. 'Oh yes!' she said. 'He's already told me he thinks you're fab and I personally think he'd be the perfect person for you.' So a meeting was arranged.

His office was a stone's throw from the Angel Tube station so very handy to walk to. I liked Stephen immediately, a born-and-bred Mancunian who trained as an actor but gave it up as, 'I was really fucking rubbish so packed it in and worked as an agent's assistant until I started my own company.'

Ooh, I thought, *he's nice and he's honest.*

I had the recording of *Mr Thomas* lined up and another play I was to appear in called *The Boys Next Door*, which would be on at the Assembly Rooms during the Edinburgh Festival and then a four-week run at the Hampstead Theatre where we'd done *Amongst Barbarians*. Stephen said he'd read *The Boys Next Door* and would've advised me not to do it, as the part was very small. I didn't agree and confidently said, 'Oh yeah, she's only in two scenes but I think she'll make an impact.'

He liked my response. 'I think I'd have a very interesting time representing you so would love you to join me if you'd be willing?'

I was, so I did, and stayed with him until he retired in 2016.

WRITER/ACTOR

Michael Custance, the producer of *Small Stages*, told me that a renowned television director had been sent all five plays for the series in the hope that he would like one of them and agree to direct. He did, and the one he chose was *Mr Thomas*. His name was Herbert Wise and he was widely known for directing all twelve episodes of a TV masterpiece from the late seventies called *I, Claudius*. I was gobsmacked. I fucking loved *I, Claudius* and couldn't quite believe this brilliant man liked my play.

We had a meeting, where he told me he was shocked when I walked into the room as he wasn't expecting me to be so young, saying in his not-too-strong Austrian accent, 'Why on earth are you writing about repressed homosexuality and alcoholism in the nineteen-fifties and not about young women of today?'

I just shrugged and gave my stock answer of, I dunno, films I suppose.

We did a run of the play for Herbie to get a sense of the blocking. It was amazing to see Matthew's beautiful set in the studio. It looked so tiny, like the corner of a very manky doll's house.

I had to make some cuts because of timing issues. In the original draft, Weaver (Ray) had a long speech about the downside of being a regular person with a job and how tedious that would be. It wasn't great, and looking back I think I was trying to emulate a wonderful speech about vending machines that was in a Tony Marchant play called *The Lucky Ones*, so I cut it. Ray was a bit peeved but hey, that's showbiz.

The recording went well and was due to be screened in January '91, exactly a year on from its opening at the Old Red.

The Boys Next Door is an American play about a group of neuro-divergent men living together in a house under the guidance of social care. I played the autistic girlfriend of one of the men. It is a sweet play with a dark undertone as one of the men, played beautifully by Marcus D'Amico, is bullied by his brute of a father, culminating with him slapping his son hard across the face, frustrated at his boy's so-called inability. It is a shocking moment in a play that for the most part is tender and funny. We sold out in Edinburgh after great reviews. We were on at 4 p.m. every day, which was perfect as it gave us free evenings to see other stuff and, more importantly, to party. I loved hanging out with Marcus and the other cast members including Allan (Alsie) Corduner and Jack Fortune.

Stephen Hatton turned up after a trip to Ireland and had read the reviews on the plane taking him to Scotland. My 'too small part' got mentioned in most, so when he met me for dinner he threw his arms around me, saying, 'You were right, she's definitely made an impact! I think our working relationship is going to be very interesting and I'm so fucking excited about the future!' We then proceeded to get mightily drunk together. He saw the show the following day and his enthusiasm hadn't waned. I was so happy that I'd taken the time before joining a new agent. Stephen 'got me' in a way others hadn't, along with the added bonus of him being a right laugh socially.

I also gained a friendly stalker. I'd noticed a bloke around my own age seemed to be wherever I was on a few occasions, taking a sly look at me when he didn't know I was looking at him.

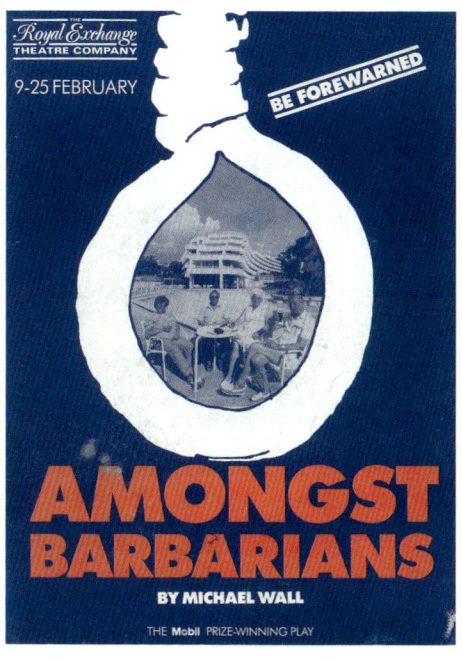

Amongst Barbarians programme

Home Free! leaflet designed
by Alison Goldfrapp

Mr Thomas leaflet designed by brother John

James Clyde as George and Ray Winstone
as Weaver in *Mr Thomas*

Great review for
Mr Thomas in *Time Out*

Me as sad, scabby Martha in *Mr Wroe's Virgins*

Waynetta visits Wayne in prison

Dad, a couple of months before
he died, holding baby Billy

Being bawdy with Max Beesley
while filming *Tom Jones*

With Mo (Laila Morse) in *Nil By Mouth*

With Gary Oldman in Cannes,
Stephen Hatton and David Thewlis
in the background

In my lovely flat with more
offers coming in

Tilly, me, Elaine and Moya holding another award I won
(can't remember what for!)

With Meryl Streep in
Dancing at Lughnasa

Taking the piss out of fame with Elaine

As Queen Mary in *Elizabeth*

Cover shoot for *Loaded* magazine

With Mel C for Comic Relief

Rehearsing a scene for
Kevin & Perry Go Large
(Perry didn't smoke!)

Linda La Hughes in
Gimme Gimme Gimme

Billy

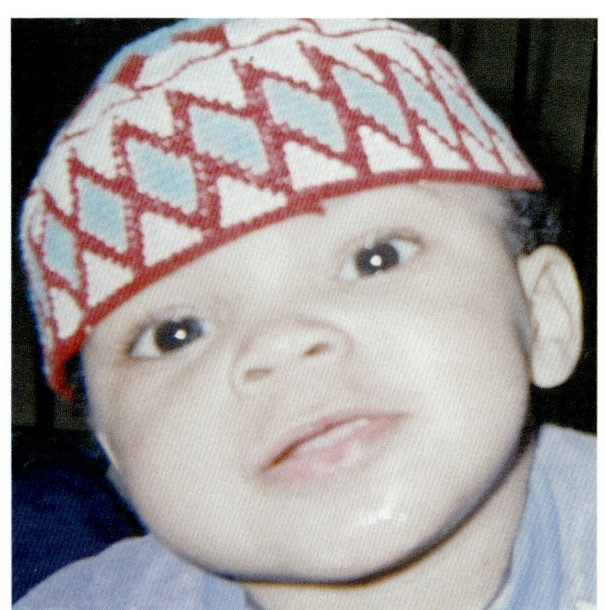

Puck aka Louis the Hat

Tilly with Georgie and Billy

My magnificent mentor, Mai Zetterling

The unparalleled Anna Scher

What the fuck does he want? Then one night, in the bar at the Gilded Balloon, I saw him leaning against a pillar, trying to look casual. I caught his eye and finally he approached me.

'Hello, you're Kathy Burke, aren't you? I saw your play, *Mr Thomas*, and *The Boys Next Door* on its first night. I thought Tina Bishop was a real person when you were on *Jonathan Ross*. I'm booked to see *The Boys Next Door* again with my mum and brother Andrew, who's autistic. Your portrayal was very accurate.'

His name was Patrick Marber and he was appearing in a comedy show along with James Macabre and living legend Jo Brand called *The Holy Cardigans* because, well, they all wore holey cardigans, I suppose.

'You're one of those St Paul's boys,' I said, which startled him because I was right. My old friend Ian Sears went to St Paul's, the private boys' school, and I'd learned to spot them a mile off.

I went to see his show, which I loved, and it was a real pleasure to meet Patrick's mum and especially his brother Andrew after they saw *The Boys Next Door*. Another lifelong friend had arrived.

The play went down well enough again at Hampstead to earn a West End transfer, but I wasn't interested in going with it. A further six months playing the same role filled me with dread, plus the bloke who played my character's boyfriend, although a brilliant actor, was a bit of a misogynistic pig and I had no desire to be in his company for another half a year, so I said thanks for a great time but no. I think another agent might've pushed me into doing it – six months' guaranteed work isn't something someone in my position would normally turn down – but Stephen was in total agreement, which was a very happy relief.

HUNGOVER II

Along with *Mr Thomas* being televised, it had also earned a Time Out Theatre Award. Marvellous! The career was going well, and I was thinking about writing another play, but the drink was taking its toll. A few things happened that finally made me stop and think.

I'd bumped into my old friend Mark Monero while mooching around Camden. We had the usual 'nice to see you's, when he asked if I still drank in the Old Red. I said yes, to which he said, not unkindly, 'I'll know where to find you when we're old and grey!' This throwaway remark had a profound effect on me. I remember walking home and thinking *I don't want that*. I don't want to be in the same place forty years down the line. Was I stuck?

Another time I was on a train heading to or from somewhere when my friend Katrin Cartlidge got on. We proceeded to have a catch-up but then she asked, under her breath, if I'd had a drink, because she could smell it on me. I was shocked. Of course I hadn't had a drink! I never drank in the day, never mind first thing in the morning, but I had, of course, been drinking the night before, and my morning shower obviously hadn't washed away the evidence. I remembered the smell could stay with Dad a while after a binge had stopped and now this was happening to me.

I didn't feel like an alcoholic, I never drank spirits, so surely I was just a social drinker who needed to cut down a bit?

A couple of times in the pub I'd had a weird feeling of anxiety. One time Perry was with me and I can't remember what happened other than he was holding my hand and making me drink some water.

'You had a panic attack, mate.'

Oh.

Then a big life change happened. I'd been wanting to move out of the big house with Dad, but certainly couldn't afford to buy anywhere, especially not in Islington, which was starting to become expensive. I'd done some bits of TV work but I'd put aside most of the money earned to get my teeth fixed, as Stephen said I couldn't put it off any longer. He was good friends with a dentist in Brighton who would provide some lovely Valium to help with the procedure without me smashing his face in, but in the meantime I really wanted to live on my own.

I met my brother John for lunch and a catch-up and he told me about a swap scheme that the council were doing. They were in desperate need of houses for families and at the time had plenty of one-bedroom flats. John said, 'Tell the old man to look into it.' So I did.

Dad was reluctant at first as he didn't really want to live on *his* own. He'd had a couple of lady friends since he'd stopped the booze but had no desire to move in with either of them at the time, so I appealed to his lefty liberalism instead, 'It's out of order, you and I are in such a big house when so many families are in need. It's bordering on morally wrong.' He had to agree and within a few months we were in our own one-bedroom flats just around the corner from each other.

I finally had the solitude I'd been craving since I was a kid. My flat, a new-build off the New North Road, had its own front door and a few steps leading up into the front room and kitchen, then another small flight of stairs that led to my bedroom and bathroom. I absolutely loved it.

I wasn't entirely on my own. I had a cool black cat called George that I'd had for a few years, and as we weren't too far from the big house the same streets were still his territory. Dad settled into his own lovely place, which was also modern but all on one level, and I think he missed having George around more than me.

Even though by this time Dad hadn't drunk for years, I never really trusted that he wouldn't succumb again, so hadn't been able to truly relax until I was in my own place. *Okay*, I thought, *you used the drink as a means to sleep through his out-of-the-blue black rages, but those haven't happened for an age, and now you're on your own they are never going to happen again, so what's the excuse?*

It was a Saturday night and Stephen and I had plans to go to a gig somewhere in Highbury. By now he had moved his office from The Angel to his home, which was just up the road from my flat. He called round so we could walk together.

'I'm not going to drink tonight,' I said.

'Oh,' he replied, 'why not?'

'I just want to see if I can do without it.'

'Okay,' he said, 'no problem.'

It was a strange night for me; the first time in my adult life that I'd been out-out without alcohol. I remember not chatting much and feeling oddly shy. When I got home I rolled a joint to take away an edgy alertness. It was so much lovelier without a drink involved. My head felt calm. *I did it*, I thought, *so maybe I can do it again?* I did the same the following night, and the night after and remained very happily alcohol-free for the next few years.

MR ENFIELD

I'd been in a couple more sketches for *French and Saunders* and once again had a great time. My favourite was a parody of the dance troupe Pan's People from the '70s. Simon and Rowland were also in it and I just remember really enjoying myself.

My Tina Bishop days were definitely over, culminating with the *Secret Policeman's* gig and I wasn't too bothered about doing any more self-created comedy characters.

Harry Enfield had made a name for himself with his brilliant comedy personas Stavros and Loadsamoney on *Friday Night Live*, which led to his own sketch show on the BBC, *Harry Enfield's Television Programme*. It was going to be jam-packed with brand-new characters including a rough married couple called Wayne and Waynetta Slob, and I was asked to audition.

It was very lovely to see Paul Whitehouse in the room with Harry. He was a writer on the show as well as performing, and I was relieved that my walking away from the Jonathan Ross show hadn't muddied his view of me.

I did a read for them, which they liked, and was offered the job there and then. I remember telling Stephen later that I didn't really get the sketch. It was just two stupid people shouting at each other, but the money was good and Harry was great so of course I'd said yes.

When it came to the rehearsal I still didn't quite understand the characters, but once we were in costume and make-up it finally clicked into place. Harry and I were both padded up and I had a very grubby velour tracksuit on top. Our make-up consisted of greasy hair and lots of spots and scabs. *Oh*, I thought, *we look very cartoony, like characters from* Viz, which I loved. *Now I get it.*

The biggest problem was trying not to laugh. Harry as Wayne looked as rough as fuck and sounded extremely thick, and it took a while to get my act together. The Slobs went down very well with the studio audience, along with the rest of the show, and the feeling by the end was that it was going to be a hit. Which it was. That first series was such a huge success it was immediately recommissioned, but after the second series I was actually worried about doing any more. I didn't want to be known as just one character, and I was already having people shouting The Slobs' catchphrase 'I am smokin' a fag!' at me in the street – especially when I was actually smoking, which of course was often.

The money was the most I'd earned so far, so I was able to finish off furnishing my little flat, including installing a washing machine, which was fucking amazing. No more boring visits to the laundrette.

DRY II

I was the healthiest I'd been since I was a kid. Life without the booze had made me shed some doughy weight and I was back to riding a brand-new bike, whizzing through London to watch films at the NFT or see new exhibitions at the National Portrait Gallery along with any theatre I could afford to see. And books! So many books I now had the time to read.

My teeth had finally been fixed by Chris the dentist in Brighton. It had been a tough journey but made so much easier by Stephen being with me every step of the way, driving me back and forth and stocking up my food cupboards with soups and other soft stuff. My new veneers felt very big in my mouth and it took a while to adjust. When Carmelita first saw them she said, 'We need to get used to them, baby-girl, cos at the moment you remind me of Esther Rantzen.' I also had to get used to smiling without covering my mouth with my hands, an automatic reaction.

Stephen also introduced me to two extremely important people in my life, Philip my accountant and Howard my financial adviser. These lovely, quietly spoken and highly intelligent men would keep me on the straight and narrow for the duration. I was now earning proper money and, apart from normal tax-deductible expenses, I wasn't interested in looking for further ways to not pay my fair share, and neither were they.

My social life was very different. I'd stopped going to the Old Red as it was too associated with getting pissed, and other pubs also lost their appeal. Going to friends' for dinner or them coming to me was now mostly on the agenda and I really liked it that way, which happily surprised me. I'd become a good cook and the girls loved my homemade veggie quiches and Greek spanakopita.

Sleep was so much better too. I still sat up till late, listening to music or watching films on video, but going to bed was something to look forward to without the slightest noise bolting me upright.

HELLO AND GOODBYE

Mai Zetterling was in London and wanted to see me. It had been about eight years since *Scrubbers*. She was staying at The Ritz or The Savoy, I can't remember which, and invited me to have tea with her. I was very early so had a browse in a bookshop beforehand, which was a favourite thing of mine to do since childhood, quiet, gentle farts still escaping from my relaxed state. I picked up a book that I'd seen many times before but had no interest in reading called *Tattoo* by Earl Thompson. I don't know why I picked it up and opened its first pages but I did and gasped at the dedication, which was to Mai Zetterling.

When I arrived at the hotel and found the designated tea area, Mai was already sat at a table waiting for me. Her tiny frame jumped up when she saw me, 'Hello, my old friend!' She beamed as we hugged and kissed but then we were rudely interrupted by the maître d', who informed us that as I was wearing jeans I wasn't allowed to stay in the restaurant. Mai huffed and puffed at the stupidity of 'these antiquated bloody rules' and said we would go to her room instead.

Once we were settled, with tea and sandwiches provided by room service, we caught up on who was doing what from the film. She was no longer seeing the boyfriend she had at the time, saying, 'He turned out to be just as rotten as the rest. I told you men were pigs.' She'd seen *Mr Thomas* on television and enjoyed it, but mirrored Herbie's comment in that, 'You should write about young women not drunk, gay men.' Flipping heck. I told her about the Earl Thompson dedication but she laughed dismissively and said he was just one of many. She asked how my dad was doing and it was lovely to tell her truthfully that he was really well. I then remembered their chat in our garden and asked what they had talked about. 'This and that,' she said, 'but I told him he wasn't to worry about you going into the profession and allow you to be a free spirit, like myself.' I asked if it was okay to smoke, 'I'd rather you didn't as I have cancer.' I was startled.

I didn't expect her to say that. Is that why she wanted to see me?

'Yes,' she said. 'I'm not going to die just yet, but once cancer gets a grip on your body you can no longer take life and time for granted.' She continued to talk about doctors and procedures and moving to London permanently, but I had become very upset so she held me and stroked my head and soothed me like a mother. 'It's okay,' she said quietly, 'I've had an incredible life and if it ends before I become feeble then so much the better.'

As we said our goodbyes she cupped my face with her hands, smiled and twinkled with her beautiful, mischievous eyes, 'Always remember to say it was *me* who found you. *Me.*' I didn't think anyone would be interested, but I always have.

A little postscript. I wondered in the here and the now if I'd remembered correctly about that book being dedicated to Mai, so I ordered a copy and it was but with a forgotten heartfeltness: 'To Mai Zetterling, whose existence is an inspiration and whose personal alchemy so helped keep me alive in a mean time.'

You and me both, mate, you and me both.

ARTSY-FARTSY

A fantastic TV exec, John Chapman, told me he'd got the rights to a novel called *Mr Wroe's Virgins* by Jane Rogers in the hope of making it for television. The story takes place in and around Lancashire and he'd grown fond of the area after producing a show at BBC Manchester called *Making Out*. He wanted to use its crew again as, 'Everything is always made in bloody London.' He gave me a copy of the book. 'There's a fantastic role for you,' he said, 'it'll take a while before I'm able to get things up and running but give it a read. The character's called Martha.'

I read it, liked it and thought no more about it until a year or so later, when Stephen told me it was happening. It would indeed be made at the studios in Manchester (well done to John for outsourcing before that was a thing) and on location in historical places such as Ashton-under-Lyne and Whitby.

The story was about a self-proclaimed prophet called John Wroe who set up a church in the 1820s, where God apparently told him he was to find comfort with seven virgins so he was gifted these by his congregation. Of course he was.

Jane Rogers's adaptation for TV was terrific, consisting of four episodes telling the story from four of the virgins' points of view. The very good actor Jonathan Pryce played Mr Wroe and Lia Williams (genius), Minnie Driver (good fun) and Kerry Fox (charmless prick) played three of the virgins, with me as the fourth, Martha.

It wasn't a given that I had the part, despite what John Chapman said. He'd brought on a new upcoming director to take the helm called Danny Boyle who had his own ideas for casting and wasn't convinced I could do the role. There was a lot of tough stuff involved for all of the actors, including nudity and sex scenes, but Martha had come from a background of brutality including rape, beatings and being treated worse than an animal. She was also mute and riddled with fleas so her hair was shaved off, which Danny wanted to happen on camera. Not a problem.

It was a lot, and it was scary, but I knew I could handle it. I discussed it non-stop with Tilly and Elaine, who were understandably worried as we'd always said we'd never do nude scenes, but I loved Martha's funny, childlike innocence of the world and really wanted to do it. I told the family, who were also concerned, particularly Dad, but Carm was matter of fact, as always, saying, 'It sounds very artsy-fartsy but sometimes you have to get out of your comfort zone and embrace new challenges, so you go for it.' After four or five auditions, Danny finally agreed with John and I was offered the part.

Its make-up designer was Ann Humphreys, who on our first meeting told me my teeth were too nice so I would have to get a false pair of manky teeth fitted. Oh the irony! Ann was wonderful and we became a proper team, particularly on our before-dawn make-up calls when I was doing nude scenes so she had to painstakingly add scabs and wounds all over my body.

The crew were great, especially sound designer Dennis Cartwright and director of photography Brian Tufano. Brian would take hours setting up lights but, after watching the rushes, John Chapman would say it was worth it despite developing stress boils the size of small tangerines on his neck.

Another actress who was involved with most of the shoot was Blackpool-born Moya Brady, small in stature but mighty in the mind, and she – along with John, Ann and Brian – was a lifesaver without whom I don't think I could have got through the job. Moya would come to my hotel room most evenings and we'd have dinner together, watch TV, smoke a much-needed spliff and, more importantly, laugh. John would sometimes join us and enjoy the piss-taking from myself and Moya about his painful-looking boils.

The set was always very quiet and over-precious. I'd use humour now and then to help get me through some of the more hardcore stuff, but this wasn't appreciated by Danny. I wasn't a twat, I knew how to behave appropriately, but sometimes a bit of light relief could help a tense atmosphere. He didn't seem to mind Jonathan Pryce cracking a few jokes.

I found the nudity and sex scenes remarkably easy once I'd got through the first one. The stuff I found difficult was trying to keep my eyes open while water was being poured over my head and down my face, or trying not to break my ankles while running barefoot over jagged rocks. The latter was impossible until Danny finally gave in and allowed the art director to place flatter fake rocks down. It was still very painful to do, but as they were covered in mud you couldn't tell the difference, and I wasn't sorry to disappoint Danny in not having actual torn and bloody feet for his vision.

After four long, hard months we were finally finished. John Chapman was delighted with my performance and incredibly proud of how I'd handled it all. And Danny? Fuck knows. There was little communication from him as it was, so I had no clue as to how he felt. Sometime later John said, 'Danny had said you wouldn't like him because he had to put you through some gruelling work, but he did get a wonderful performance from you.' This gave me the biggest laugh yet. I wasn't an idiot, I *knew* it would be gruelling from reading the script a million times. I achieved the 'wonderful performance' on my own, with guidance and encouragement from Ann, Brian, Moya and John himself. Danny was a mystery to me and reminded me of a supercilious priest from my childhood.

I won an Royal Television Society award for my efforts and a great friend in Moya, but once it had been screened I was very glad to see the back of it.

A TERRIBLE TOUR

I was now being offered jobs without having to audition, and among them was the part of Toinette the maid in a touring production of Molière's *The Hypochondriac*. It was a great play and a great part, but a big fucking disaster. It was a terrible production and I was terrible in it. I wouldn't have bothered to include it in this book if it didn't involve a particular incident and a few noteworthy people, the first of whom being James Dreyfus. He was brilliantly funny in the play and we buzzed while working together, even though we couldn't get through rehearsing our first scene without laughing, leading our frustrated director to snap, 'Go back to the start, you two!'

As we headed back to where our marked-out entrance was, I side-mouthed to James under my breath, 'Here we go, babe, back to cunt corner.' He howled, we bonded and this, unsurprisingly, became our catchphrase.

Debra Gillett, a petite, bouncy-haired blondie from the middle-class bit of Bury in Manchester, was our leading lady. I liked Debs immediately. She was a brilliant actress with a great lightness of touch and was also good fun to be around. She, me and another actress, Avril Clarke, stuck together like glue, sharing digs and slagging off our leading man. Avril was very naughty with a posh throaty voice, and her bemoaning of, 'How hideous this production is!' was hilarious and gave us much-needed light relief. This job was so fucking stressful, and my performance so bad and unsure of itself, that I contracted shingles. Shingles?! What the fuck?

Another actor who was suffering along with us was Kevin

215

Elyot, who would later become an incredibly successful writer, most notably with his award-winning play *My Night with Reg*. Kevin was sweet and funny but full of melancholy, which wasn't only because of the job. (I think it's okay to write this next bit as those involved have since passed away or are hopefully too old to care.)

We were nearing the end of the tour and Kevin was staying in the same digs as myself and the girls. We sat in its tiny kitchen after the show one night, Kevin, Debs and Avril quaffing the wine, me puffing on a joint, when the chat turned to love. Kevin was reluctant to join in at first, but Avril was a skilled poker, 'Come on, Kevin, what's your story?' His reluctance was understandable when he told us the love of *his* life had died a few years before, but what made things worse was that his lover had a (male) life partner, meaning Kevin was the secret lover.

'Jack never met any of my friends, nor I any of his,' he said. 'I put up with it because I loved him and being with him when we could was enough for me. But then he got sick and he called and said he loved me deeply and was sorry but this is where it ends. I couldn't even go to his funeral.'

We were very moved by his story and Kevin himself had become teary at the telling. Avril did another gentle poke, 'Who was he?'

Kevin laughed, saying, 'No one *you* would know. He was American and not in the business. That's the worst of it all, I don't know another single soul who knew him, which at times can make me feel very lonely or sometimes quite mad, like he never existed.'

I don't know why but something was niggling at me, so I took hold of the poking baton. 'What did he do?' I asked.

Kevin sighed, a little impatiently now. 'Like I said, he wasn't in our industry, he worked as a lecturer in London.'

So then I asked, 'Did he lecture in film studies?'

Kevin was shocked and looked at me with wide-eyed disbelief, 'Yes.'

'I knew him, Kev,' I said. 'Not very well, we weren't mates as such, but he taught me at further education college.'

'Yes,' said Kevin, trying to catch his breath. 'He taught at Kingsway.'

Now there was no doubt, I recalled that last time I had seen Jack, at the screening of *Scrubbers*, and the man he didn't introduce me to.

'That was me,' said Kevin. '*That was me!*'

When the job finally came to its never-ending end, Kevin and I didn't become friends, but we would sometimes bump into each other at press nights and the like. He'd give me a hug and we'd share a secret smile and I would always say, 'Jack sends his love.'

To which he would always reply, 'He sends his love to you too.'

A FABULOUS TIME

Jennifer Saunders got in touch. She had written a sitcom for the BBC called *Absolutely Fabulous*, starring herself along with Julia Sawalha, Jane Horrocks and living legends June Whitfield and Joanna Lumley. Jen wanted me to play the part of a magazine editor called Magda. On the first script read-through we sat chatting for ages, as Jen always took things up to the wire and was still in an office, photocopying. When she eventually arrived in the rehearsal room, greeted by piss-taking claps and whistles, the scripts were hot to the touch.

The silly and pretentious world of the fashionistas was new to me and most of the cast. I kept hearing a woman's name being mentioned so I turned to Joanna and asked who Jen was talking about. Her reply in that beautiful, soft, buttery voice was without a hint of judgement, 'She's who your character is based on, darling.'

The only note I can remember Jen giving me was, 'Say your lines as quickly as possible.' Magda had brilliantly scathing and offensive stuff to say, and Jen felt the quicker they came out the harder it would be for the TV police to cut them.

It was strange not having Dawn around, and for the first couple of days I kept looking for her, but it was very nice hanging out with Harriet Thorpe and Helen Lederer for most of the time and having lovely designer clothes to wear. The set was adorned with very expensive bird of paradise flowers, which I had never seen before, and I was chuffed when the props guy let me take some home at the end of the recording.

I received a card from Jen a few weeks later that said something along the lines of, 'Who knows what people will make of *Ab Fab*, it'll probably be a flash in the pan but thanks a million for taking part.'

Her sparkling, modest brain had no clue it was to become the phenomenon it was.

WHAT A SHAME

I was asked by the Royal Exchange, Manchester, if I'd like to be its writer in residence. This felt like a great idea as it had been three years since *Mr Thomas* and I still hadn't got round to writing a second play, so maybe this would give me the time and motivation. The only problem was I would have to find my own accommodation and workspace as there wasn't an office available for me to work in. I said to Stephen, 'How the hell can I be in residence when there isn't one?' He would look into it some more, but in the meantime Mike Leigh wanted to meet me about a play he would be directing at the Theatre Royal Stratford East. There was no script of course as, like his TV and film work, it would be developed through improvisation. I was a bit torn as the dates meant I couldn't take up the Exchange's offer, so it would have to be one or the other. Mike – along with Ken Loach and Alan Clarke – was one of the few directors back then who regularly used working-class actors and was someone I really wanted to work with, so in the end I thought I'd be daft to miss out on the opportunity. The writing would have to wait.

I enjoyed working with Mike, his process was different and interesting and I really liked my eventual character, a street urchin named Nellie. After a few weeks of rehearsal, the play was called *It's a Great Big Shame!*, after a music-hall song from the Victorian era. This was because the first half, which my character was a part of, was set in the early 1890s, while the second half had the contemporary setting of the early 1990s. This felt exciting, as Mike had never done a period piece before. As usual, getting it together was all top secret. Moya had worked with Mike on his film *Life Is Sweet*, so knew she couldn't dig too much, but during a phone call she asked for just a hint as to what was happening, then laughed like a drain when I said, 'All I'm going to say is my character's wearing a flat cap and smoking a pipe.'

The play went down okay I think, but by this time I'd stopped reading reviews, so who knows, but it was sold out for the majority of its performances. It was a difficult time for me. About halfway through rehearsals Dad came over for a cuppa. He'd spotted blood in his urine so had an appointment at Bart's Hospital to have his prostate checked. 'Do you want me to come with you?' I asked.

But, 'I've already been,' he said, 'I should get the results in a couple of weeks.'

I made reassuring noises that it was a good thing he'd been checked early and I was sure everything would be okay, trying to convince myself as well as him, but when the results came through it wasn't okay. It was cancer.

A lot of what followed is a blur.

I carried on with the job as best I could. We were halfway through the run when there was a note waiting for me when we finished a midweek matinee. 'Your dad wants you to phone him.' I went to one of the theatre offices, my heart pounding. I didn't know what I was expecting him to say as there was an appointment lined up with a consultant the following week, so maybe it was about something else, something trivial? I was shocked when he picked up the call. He was drunk. I hadn't heard or seen him drunk for nearly ten years. My body went into spasms, I gripped the edge of the table to keep myself steady.

'What's going on? Why are you drinking?!'

He laughed. 'Why do you *think* I'm drinking? I'm dying, Kathy.'

'You're *not* dying!' I snapped. 'There'll be treatments but you'll fuck it all up if you drink!'

'I just need to ask you something.' He was oddly calm. 'I just want you to be with me when the time comes, just be with me, that's all I'm asking.'

I didn't know what to say. When I was a little kid I was so terrified of him that if he hadn't returned home for a couple of days I'd often pray for him to be dead but then the sound of the key in the door . . .

I was nearing the end of my twenties and had finally reached a point of trust and, dare I say, love, but now I was angry and frightened all over again. I knew there was no point in berating him further, realising he was probably far more frightened than me.

'I'll come and see you in the morning,' I said.

'And when the time comes?'

'I'll be there,' I said.

A MADNESS

It's very difficult writing about this time period. I've thought about it over the years, but to sit in it, to relive feelings, is hard.

I'd fallen in love with someone who wasn't good for me. The who and whys are not important, but the timing is relevant because I was distracted and I've had to live with the guilt of this.

The relationships I had before and after were with good men. I'd experienced the pain of unrequited love of course, but cruelty had never played a part. Dark mind games were not something I'd been subjected to, nor being laughed at and called a fool. I was told I wasn't wanted, yet at the same time referred to as a soulmate. Before we met I was confident and strong and happy, but now I was in a continuous state of flux. I tried so hard to not be in love. To not care. I knew they were undeserving. I knew they were getting a sadistic kick, but there was an unstop-pable force. As old as time. I was a cliché. I was embarrassed and I felt ashamed. My precious time had been wasted.

JOHN PATRICK

The end of 1993 was full of darkness but there was a beautiful light peeping through. Tilly and Ade had a baby, my godson, Billy. They were living in a lovely garden flat not too far from mine and I saw them as often as possible.

I would see Dad for a cuppa or get him a bit of shopping in as well as going with him to the odd appointment at the hospital. He didn't drink again. He came with me to visit Tilly and baby Bill. The last photo I took of him, Billy is in his arms.

There was a knock on my flat door one night. It was late, I wasn't expecting anyone, so I didn't answer. The next day Dad told me it had been him and his nephew, who had surprised him with a visit from America. His brother Joe's son turned up out of the blue, who Dad hadn't seen since Joe's funeral in 1981. Dad wasn't a believer but the visit felt like a messenger and he took great comfort from this.

In March 1994, I received the news that Mai Zetterling had died. I phoned Dad to tell him and of course I became upset. I'm glad, though, because I don't think he'd heard or seen me upset for years, and he knew and I knew that I was also crying for him, which again gave him comfort.

Now it was April. The brilliant writer Dennis Potter had a cancerous tumour and gave a televised interview with Melvyn Bragg where he talked candidly about life and his imminent death. In it he spoke about his serenity and appreciation of life and the tree in his garden whose blossoms were now to him, 'the whitest, frothiest, blossomest blossoms that there ever could be.'

My phone rang as the transmission ended and I knew it was Dad.

'Were you watching Dennis Potter?' he asked.

I said yes.

And he continued, 'He was able to say what I'm feeling. I'm unable to express myself like him but I feel like he was speaking on my behalf. Does that make sense, Kathy?'

'It makes total sense, Dad,' I said.

A week or so later there was a bad night when he was in a bad way, so I called the doctor and she called the ambulance.

His last couple days were at St Bart's. It was a peaceful death and we were with him. Me holding Dad's hand, John holding mine, and I watched as the invisible flutter left his body.

AFTERWARDS

Barry and Carm arrived at the hospital just as I was leaving.

'He's gone,' I said.

'Thank God there was no prolonged agony for him,' said Carm.

The funeral was a good one. Dad had instructed us as to how it would be. I gave the eulogy, which included thanks to the Galvins and the Corcorans for their help over the years. He didn't want any of his old drinking buddies to attend and he wanted the wake to be at the Old Red Lion. 'Make sure that all the food provided is from Marks and Spencer's.' So it was.

About a week or so later John, Barry and I cleared out his flat and I kept an Ireland rugby shirt.

Ronan was out of the country but sent me some flowers. Of all my acting friends, Ronan was Dad's favourite to watch. Perry sent a card that said, 'I noticed Mai Zetterling passed away just a few weeks before your dad so I like to think she was putting the kettle on in time for his arrival.'

The months that followed were quiet and tearful and I spent as much time with baby Billy as I could. His newness and wonder at the world, which I could see in his beautiful eyes, mirrored the musings of Dennis Potter and so too therefore my dad's. And I took great comfort from this.

PART THREE

BACK TO WORK

I was in a TV film for the BBC and I can't even remember the name. Then I did a small cameo in an episode of a new series about a gang of northern binmen called *Common as Muck*, starring Edward Woodward, Michelle Holmes and Neil Dudgeon. Its writer, Billy Ivory, wanted to explore my character more so I was asked by the exec, my old pal John Chapman, if I would be in the whole of its second series. I'd become friends with Dudgeon when we worked together in a play a couple of years before and the producer was a fantastic woman called Catherine Wearing, so I said yes. Which I shouldn't have as I wasn't emotionally stable.

I'd been to see a doctor after Dad's departure and the bad love and was told I had suppressed a clinical breakdown. Medication was offered and rest, but I took neither and ploughed on with the work. It was a distraction and I liked being back in Manchester with the *Mr Wroe's* crew and a great director called Metin Hüseyin. Ann Humphreys was once again our make-up designer and she took real pleasure in sending me to a posh hairdresser and tanning shop, 'Eeh, it's lovely to have you looking so nice after all those scabs on *Mr Wroe*!' It was a good job with good people especially Dudgeon, Metin and Catherine, and despite a lot of tears I had a good time.

It was also around this time the Harry Enfield team got back in touch about another series, but I said no. As I've said, I didn't want to become known for just one character, and The Slobs were all that was being offered.

A few days later I was up The Angel getting some shopping when a black cab pulled up beside me.

'Oi, Kath! Get in here!' It was Paul Whitehouse, so I got in. 'Why don't you want to do the show, babe?!'

I surprised us both by bursting into tears (flipping heck, were they ever going to fucking stop?!). 'They only want me to do The Slobs, Paul, and there's a bit more to me than that.'

He said they were still in the early writing stages and he'd have a chat with Harry as, 'He's absolutely gutted you don't want to come back, but now I know why I think it'll be easy to sort out. Bear with me, babe.'

He gave me a ring the following week. Among Harry's characters in the first series was a kid called Little Brother, who Harry now wanted to change into a teenager. Paul suggested that my once-tried character Perry, from the Jonathan Ross show, could be the teenager's friend. How would I feel about that?

'Oh yes,' I said, 'that sounds like a lovely idea.'

'Great!' said Paul. 'There'll be some other stuff for you as well but just wanted to check about Perry. We'll get back to you!'

I went for lunch with Stephen. He was worried about my mental health. I'd lost a lot of weight, was pretty low-spirited most of the time and spent days off walking aimlessly around London. I assured him I'd be okay, I just needed more time and distance from the bad, sad stuff.

Because of the aforementioned weight loss, and to some extent my sadness and vulnerability, I was getting a lot of attention from men. There were declarations from some very lovely people, but I wasn't up for it. I didn't trust anyone, or myself, and the odd fling was all I could muster. Let's just crack on with the work.

Stephen said Harry Enfield's producer had been in touch. Along with The Slobs and teenagers Kevin and Perry, Harry also wanted me to pair with him as a Lovely Wobbly Randy Old Lady, and a snooty couple from the Midlands called Stanley and Pam, whose catchphrase was 'We're considerably richer than yow'. As Paul was also going to be playing more characters, the show was now going to be called *Harry Enfield and Chums*, and Paul and I would be in the opening credits along with Harry.

Blimey, I thought, *all hail to the power of saying no.*

MORE BRIGHT LIGHTS

Marianne Jean-Baptiste had been in the Mike Leigh play but was in the second half set in the 1990s so we didn't spend much time together. I got to know her properly some months later when Stephen had a party because she too was a client of his. Fuck me, that man had impeccable taste.

She was there with her then boyfriend, now husband, Evan, who at that time was a ballet dancer. Classy. The three of us settled on the floor in the corner of Stephen's front room and talked and talked and talked until everyone else had left and the dawn was breaking. We continued in this vein every time we met during the subsequent years, either at mine or their lovely flat in East Dulwich. Not only was Marianne an outstanding actress, writer, painter and composer, she was also a brilliant cook. I'd started to eat fish while working on *Mr Wroe's Virgins* because my body craved the extra protein, so was now a pescatarian, and Marianne's sea bass with ginger, lime and chillies was a requested favourite.

I knew Liza Tarbuck from the Old Red. Perry had worked with her and Gill (Emma) Wray on the sitcom *Watching* and, along with fellow Scousers Robbie Jarvis, Eggsy and Gary, she had become a regular. We had always got on but after Dad died she started calling more to check I was doing okay. She'd drive us up to Hampstead Heath, where we'd go on long walks with her dog, Gus, who I surprisingly wasn't scared of, or I'd go to her flat in Archway where her best mate, Kevin Eldon, would often be. They were both really funny while also being kind and understanding about my grief but annoyingly didn't patronise and still slaughtered me at Scrabble.

I knew Joe Wright from Anna Scher's and he was also one of the gang from the kids table at the Old Red. I bumped into him on Upper Street one day after he'd visited his lovely mum Lyndie, as he too had lost his dad a few months before my loss of mine. He'd been at film school and had two short films under his belt, so I said he should pop round for a cuppa as I'd love to see them, which he did. I thought his films were really great and could tell he was an exceptional talent. We'd go for long walks into town or down to the South Bank and he'd ask about my inspirations so I'd tell him about the films I loved, along with books and artwork. I thought I was just being a friend but he said he also considered me a mentor and this made me feel better about myself, as if I was worthwhile and I felt valued. It wasn't always a serious time as I'd started drinking again to numb the pain, so we also liked getting roaring drunk and dancing till we were spent. He was like my little brother.

I showed Joe's films to Catherine Wearing, who called him in for a meeting and offered him a job directing a four-part drama there and then. Joe always says this is what kickstarted his career and still thanks me for that to this day. Too right.

MR HARVEY

A few months before the bad, sad days, Tilly and I had been to see a brilliant play at the Bush Theatre in Shepherd's Bush called *Beautiful Thing*. Our friend Patricia Kerrigan was in it and had told us while she was in rehearsal, 'I don't usually insist friends come along to see me in stuff but this play is special and the writer is special. He's an ex-teacher from Liverpool called Jonathan Harvey and I think you'll both love it.' So we booked.

We were scanning the glowing reviews pinned up outside the theatre before going in when a very smiley young man with a soft Scouse accent introduced himself, 'Hiya, you're Patricia's friends, I'm Jonathan, I wrote the play.' After we said our hellos and well done on your reviews, we went upstairs to the tiny theatre space with its packed auditorium.

It was one of the most joyous plays I'd ever seen. Hettie Macdonald's direction was sublime, and Patricia and the rest of the cast, including an incredibly talented and rather handsome young actor called Jonny Lee Miller, were excellent.

By the following year or so, though, I was broken. I was hardly going out when Ronan asked me to go to the Bush with him to see another play that I can't remember. Dominic Dromgoole was the artistic director and he came over to say hello. I knew Dom from the Old Red. *Mr Thomas* had given the place an interesting boost, leading to Dom's first professional directing job being there, along with Stephen Daldry and Katie Mitchell. Just three of the future magnificent theatre stars 'Whispering' Ken McClymont had taken a chance on. What a quiet genius.

Dom asked how I was doing and I replied, rather gloomily,

that I had apparently suppressed a clinical breakdown and was feeling like a piece of shit. Oh. Ronan was worried about me expressing myself so freely and, after Dominic left our table, said, 'Be careful, Kath, this business doesn't like people being unwell.' He was right and I appreciated his kind concern but I honestly couldn't care less.

A couple of days later, Dominic called me. 'Hello, darling,' he said, 'I've been very worried about you since I saw you the other night, why are you so troubled?' So I filled him in on all the gory details, despite the warning from Ronan. He listened patiently then surprised me by saying something absolutely no other person in a position of power would say, 'You poor thing, I'm so sorry about your dad and that horrible person fucking with your beautiful mind. I think it would do you the world of good if you directed a play. I've got the latest one here by Jonathan Harvey. It's terrific fun and I think you'd do a lovely job with it. Can I send it to you?'

Jonathan and I clicked immediately. He was still riding high on the success of *Beautiful Thing*, which had since had a tour and a run at the Donmar Warehouse with a new cast *and* was in the pre-production stages for a film version. You'd think this would turn a brand-new writer into a bit of a big-headed prick, but not our Jonathan, who was daft and funny and beautifully naughty. I had to learn not to look at him during production meetings, when he'd try to make eye contact while salaciously eating a banana.

The play was called *Boom Bang-a-Bang* and was an ensemble piece about a group of friends who gathered in a flat for their annual watching of the Eurovision Song Contest. It wasn't going to change the world in the way *Beautiful Thing* had but was still, as Dominic said, terrific fun.

Our cast included Jane Hazlegrove, my pals Robbie Jarvis and Elaine Lordan, and a very young Francis Lee who would go on to have great success as a writer-director with his films *God's Own Country* and *Ammonite*. I think Jane is the only actor I've directed who I never had to give notes to as her natural instincts were always right.

The cast got on well, a bit too well, as once we were up and running they, along with Jonathan and half of the audience, would party till the early hours in a tiny Polish restaurant across the road from the theatre that would grace them with a lock-in. I would join them now and then and I'd oblige someone (can't remember who) who liked to roll me up in a floor rug then roll me out again.

Dominic was chuffed as we sold out and had great reviews. A standout one for me described Elaine's character as having 'legs from heaven and a voice from Billingsgate'.

The job was a perfect tonic. It helped me get back on my feet, and my mind was beginning to feel like my own again thanks to darling Dominic and naughty Jonathan.

EARLY THIRTIES

I was doing okay. *Harry Enfield and Chums* and *Absolutely Fabulous* were both big hits and it felt like everyone in the country was watching and saying their respective catchphrases. The Slobs were still incredibly popular, and Harry and I had a great time playing them, but there was one sketch I was a little worried about. In it, Waynetta was broody for a baby but, 'I want a *brown* baby like the other mums on the estate!' Was this a bit dodgy? Maybe a bit racist even? I phoned Carmelita and read out the sketch. She laughed and said it was fine by her as, 'We brown babies *are* the most beautiful so of course Waynetta would want one.'

A favourite sketch I did with Harry involved my character, Perry, turning up at Kevin's house after visiting Manchester, where he'd developed the walk and talk of Liam Gallagher from Oasis. I'd told Harry and Paul about the times when I arrived home from Wigan as a kid sporting the accent. They thought this was great so turned the story into the sketch.

We had to record Perry's entrance a few times as the roar from the studio audience was too much for our sound engineer to bear. This sketch still does the rounds on social media now and then, especially if Oasis are in the news. I also really enjoyed playing The Toddlers, a tiny brother and sister duo who were loosely based on Lily and Alfie Allen, who Harry was stepdad to for a while. The set was brilliant as it consisted of extra-extra-large furniture and prop pieces to help our characters look small. It was like being in a favourite movie of mine as a kid from the '50s called *The Incredible Shrinking Man*.

Comic Relief came round again so Dawn and Jen asked if

I'd take part in a sketch along with Lulu and Llewella Gideon parodying new girl group the Spice Girls. Our group was called the Sugar Lumps and we made a video where we all mimed along to the song 'Who Do You Think You Are'. The Spice Girls were just on the cusp of global domination and they were great fun. Sporty and Posh were my favourites.

I was now being referred to as a comedienne, which irked me a bit as I'd never done stand-up and had for the most part done straight acting. The newspapers liked putting people in particular boxes and I was now in the 'funny' one without any real acknowledgement of my past work. Lazy twats.

Among the straight roles was Christine in Patrick Marber's new version of Strindberg's *Miss Julie* renamed *After Miss Julie*.

Patrick had made a writing name for himself with his hit play *Dealer's Choice*, but this piece was originally written for television. We had a good time but the standout happening was that I, in a roundabout way, introduced Patrick to his future wife and mother of his children, my friend Debra Gillett, from the terrible tour. A few years later Patrick forgot to thank me during his wedding speech for making his life a whole lot better so it's great to put it down in writing now. You're welcome!

I was more than happy with the money I was making but it didn't cross my mind to go on holiday. The summer after Dad passed away, Dawn French had invited myself and a small handful of pals and kids – including Bob Pugh and daughter Scarlett and new friend Gregor Truter – down to Cornwall for a week or so. This was way before Dawn lived there permanently so instead she'd rented a beautiful house in Marazion with a perfect view of St Michael's Mount. It was a lovely time. I hadn't seen that much of Cornwall when I was touring with Paines Plough apart from looking out the van window, but this time I fell in love with the place and promised myself I would go back someday.

I don't know why I never took myself off somewhere. Work was a major factor, and I wasn't keen on the heat, so time off was usually spent at home catching up with pals, which I enjoyed, or spending time with Billy, which I *loved*.

A friend from the Old Red, Tony Simpson (acting name Jay Simpson) was a regular visitor to my flat and would sometimes look after cool cat George if I was away working. He'd been helping Gary Oldman with a screenplay that Gary was writing and hoping to direct, and said Gary had asked after me. I hadn't been in touch with Gary for years. I felt he'd become a bit of an arsehole when things started to happen for him, and we had inevitably drifted apart. He went off to Hollywood and became the star he deserved to be, so I didn't think he'd given me a second thought, but Tony said on the contrary. 'I think he really wants you to be in the film. He asks about you a lot and he's been very cool and smart during the time I've spent with him.'

I said something along the lines of, nah, not interested, but Tony pushed on.

'It's a fucking great script, mate. He stopped the booze a while back and he's actually extremely focused.'

Sometime later Stephen took me for lunch and said he'd been sent and read Gary's script, 'It's fantastic,' he said, 'I mean *really* fantastic. I've never read such realistic dialogue and the part he wants you to play is wonderful.' I ummed and ahhed like a spoiled twat. I really wanted to do more theatre directing after *Boom Bang-a-Bang* and finally get on with writing another fucking play. This was the only time I remember Stephen getting cross with me and putting his foot down. 'You can't dismiss it without reading the bloody thing! If you *read* it then tell me no then *fine*, but I think you'd be very foolish if you don't give it a look and I'd be a terrible fucking agent if I just said okay, sure, whatever you want.'

So I read it and Stephen, along with Tony, was right. Not only was it fantastic, it was probably the best script I'd ever read. The rat-a-tat dialogue peppered with perfectly placed profanity was scary but often hilarious, and the chaos that alcoholism and drug abuse can bring to a family was truthful and recognisable. Growing up, I loved the films of Ken Loach and John Cassavetes, and *Nil By Mouth* read like a combination of both.

The part of Val had been offered to me, along with Ray Winstone as Raymond, Jamie Foreman as Mark, Edna Doré as Grandma Kath, and Charlie Creed-Miles as Val's brother Billy. It was of course very nice to be offered the role but I felt it important I meet Gary before I accepted. So I did.

He was like a different person. The last time I had seen Gary, some ten years or so before, he was flash, arrogant and, well, drunk. Now he was quietly spoken, measured and gentle. I remembered the difference in myself as a drinker then non-drinker, a shyness had taken the place of bravado, and it appeared this had happened with him too. We had a very lovely chat. He said the shoot would be incredibly tough, but rather than the attitude of Danny Boyle, which was all *you're going to hate me*, Gary said, 'I know you're up to it, but I promise I'll look after you. If you ever start to feel worried or scared we'll just stop until you feel okay. Communication is key.' So I said yes.

We had a few days' rehearsal combined with costume fittings

and make-up tests with our wonderful designer Fae Hammond. An actress was on board to play my mum, Janet. She looked very young, not that much older than myself, which I was secretly concerned about but said nothing as it wasn't my business. Gary phoned one evening, however, and said pretty much the same and that he was sorry but he was going to have to recast, and he asked what I thought about his big sister, Maureen. Mo, as she preferred to be called, had originally been given the job as my driver and I found her quite fascinating. She'd had a rough life in her younger days and told me some pretty hardcore stories on a couple of our journeys from north to south-east London and back again.

The following morning a different driver picked me up and Mo was already nervously waiting in the rehearsal room. We read through some scenes together and did a couple of improvisations. She was understandably a bit unsure here and there and, as she said herself, was 'absolutely bricking it' but her line delivery and timing were terrific and hilarious so Gary gave her the job and ultimately the greatest opportunity of her life.

When Ray and I did half a day's rehearsal together, Gary gave me a key note that helped with my entire performance. We were improvising a scene that was just chatting in a pub or some such. The film ends with my character Val giving a little speech, her finally having space to talk among the men's overbearing chatter, and during the improvisation I had this version of Val in my mind but Gary stopped me. 'You're making her too sharp, we see that sharpness in her at the end but up until that point she's punch-drunk.' Punch-drunk. It was simple and it was enough.

NIL BY MOUTH

On the first day of filming, Charlie Creed-Miles came into my tiny trailer and said he would be using method acting for the film. My heart sank. I hated this indulgent bollocks and was worried others might follow suit. I found Ray in Make-up and asked if he knew about Charlie's intentions. 'Yeah,' he said nonchalantly, 'when he told me I said okay, now go to the shop and get me some fags.'

Oh that's brilliant, I thought. Charlie's character was lower status than mine, Ray's and Jamie's, so I went to find him and told him to go to the shop for me too. After just a day of us all ordering him around, he rather sheepishly informed us on day two that he'd gone off the idea. Fantastic. Now we could all get on with the job in hand.

Mo was understandably still very nervous. Not only had she never acted before but she had the added pressure of not wanting to let her brother down. I happily took her under my wing, which helped us bond and stopped me indulging in my own nerves.

It was a low-budget, independent movie, which meant the schedule was pretty tough and the conditions were grim. The flats we filmed in were empty and waiting for demolition, which was great for noise control but they were absolutely freezing, which led to me getting pleurisy so I had to step away for a few days. Looking back, this really helped, as Gary and brilliant director of photography Ron Fortunato had extra time to shoot some beautiful cinematic footage of Charlie's character, Billy, wandering through the estate's bleak and foggy atmosphere.

242

Gary was really up against it most of the time because of budget constraints, and there were a couple of rocky days when the whole shoot was under threat of being shut down. But he persisted and pushed through.

My character, Val, had to go through some rough stuff. Her being dragged out of bed by Ray's character and then beaten to a pulp by him was one of the roughest and the hardest for the eventual audience to watch. It was a breeze to shoot, though, because I was safe. Gary made sure I was safe and so did Ray. I wasn't hurt in the slightest. I wasn't bullied, I wasn't given dirty looks if I tried to lighten the mood, instead I was twinkled at with warmth and gratitude. I found it a very easy shoot overall. It was exhilarating and satisfying.

I didn't go out drinking with the cast and crew at all. The shoot was heavy enough without the extra burden of a hangover. This irked Ray somewhat, leading him to ask one day at wrap, 'Are you ever gonna come to the bloody pub with us? What you going home for? You're behaving as if you're married!'

To which I replied, 'I *am* married, babe, to *myself*!'

I remember closing the door to my lovely flat when I'd get home each evening, reflecting on poor, unfortunate Val and think, *There but for the grace of God go I.* Jonathan remembers coming over for dinner a couple of times during the shoot and was shocked when he saw the film as he had no clue I was involved with something so hard-hitting, saying, 'You were in really good spirits and didn't talk about it being tough. You would just recall funny stuff that happened in the day, cook my tea and have a laugh.'

When we finally wrapped on the film, we all breathed a sigh of relief that we'd got through it without being shut down. Gary gave me some flowers and a hug and thanked me for trusting him, and I left happy with the fact that I'd spent the last few months with some of the best actors and the best director I'd ever worked with.

FAME II

I was drinking again but not in the way I'd drunk before. I didn't drink every night, only on the odd occasions I went out. I was starting to get recognised, which I found pretty nerve-wracking, so was using it as a crutch to get through. I thought when I was younger that fame would be a marvellous thing, but for me it really wasn't. I found it, for the most part, embarrassing. If I was out with friends I'd spend a lot of the time chatting with strangers who wanted to say hello. Not wanting to be thought of as a cunt, those people had to take priority – so I started to have nights out *in* instead, either at my flat or friends'. Marianne, Evan and I would quaff champagne, particularly on the very exuberant night we found out Marianne had been nominated for an Oscar, but then I realised I was allergic to the fermented grape so went back to my old favourite, Stella.

After recording *Harry Enfield and Chums* or *Ab Fab* there would be drinks in the green room, but I never stayed as I preferred to get home as quickly as possible and have a little smoke instead. I rarely invited people to the recordings so I wasn't spoiling anyone's fun. It's funny because members of the public would often ask me how Harry was. Or, 'What's Harry up to?' I liked H but, apart from a couple of lunches, we didn't knock about together.

Being recognised in the street was okay during the daytime as people were usually very nice, but at night with a drink inside them it could sometimes feel a bit scary and I'd have to be on my guard, which wasn't very enjoyable. I'd occasionally go to the members-only club Groucho, but then you'd just get other famous people, usually off their nut on coke, coming over and chatting shit, so you'd long for a pub full of normals.

Black cab drivers always wanted a chat. They would often open with, 'Ooh, Islington, eh? You moving up in the world?' This would piss me off as I explained for the millionth time I was born and bred, thank you very much! And then we'd chat on about house prices and the like. I wasn't always in the mood to talk, which they could sense so would leave me alone to my own thoughts. On one of my non-chatty occasions something quite extraordinary happened.

It was late afternoon and I was heading home from the West End after a meeting or something and hailed a taxi. I'm always polite but definitely gave the please-let's-not-chat vibe when the driver recognised me. We trundled along the whole journey in a happy silence, but as we turned into my road a strong sulphur-type smell, much akin to something electrical burning, started to happen so I alerted the driver, 'I think there's something wrong with your cab, mate, there's a weird burning smell.' The driver pulled over, got out and opened the passenger door. The smell had gone. I told him to turn the engine back on as it was definitely something electrical; he did, but there was nothing. I said that's odd and that I hadn't imagined it *blah blah blah*.

I got out of the cab and was getting together some cash to pay when he said, 'I could tell you didn't want to talk earlier but my wife would be very annoyed if I didn't tell you she used to be a big fan of yours.'

I said something along the lines of yes, sorry about that, I'm not always in the mood for talking – and then, hang on, what do you mean by *used* to be? Has she gone off me? Have I done something wrong?

He gave a half-hearted smile and said, 'Oh no, sorry, no, I'm afraid she died.' I was taken aback. He looked so young, no more than early thirties.

'Oh mate,' I said, 'I'm so sorry! How on earth . . .?' And then I thought, *Fuck that, we can't stand in the street talking about this*, and for some reason took the burning smell as a sign from his wife urging me to talk to him. 'Come on,' I said. 'Let's go in mine and have a cup of tea.'

Now he was the one taken aback and said he couldn't possibly inconvenience me, so I asked if he had kids. Yes, he replied, two. I told him I had lost my mum when I was a baby, so then he said, yes please, he could actually do with having a cuppa and a chat.

We sat for an hour or so. This poor young man, with two kids under the age of ten, had woken up one morning to find his wife not asleep but dead in the bed next to him from a brain aneurysm. It had happened a few months before and this was his first week back working in the cab. He talked about the shock, about how amazing his wife was, how worried he was about his kids and that his sister or sister-in-law had offered to look after them for a bit but he was determined to do this himself as he didn't want the kids to feel like he was deserting them. As I listened I realised he was probably the same age our dad was when Mum died.

'I think it's important you spend some time away from your kids,' I said, 'so you can grieve properly and they can do the same without worrying about you, which they will be. Take yourself away somewhere for a while and let your support system step in. I wish our dad had done that.'

He took this in, nodded and said he'd think about it.

We said our goodbyes, he thanked me for the chat and I wished him all the very best. I often think about him and his now-grown kids. I hope he took the advice given from my own experience, as I look back on that afternoon as a good day to be 'famous'.

TALLY-HO!

I'd never ridden a horse of course and now I was clip-clopping around a stables atop a small yet mighty stallion called Spud. It was in preparation for the role of Honour, the maid in a new BBC version of Henry Fielding's *Tom Jones*. Frances de la Tour, a hero of mine, was watching from the sidelines and called out to me in her magnificent, distinctive voice, 'You look fab on that!'

I wasn't really interested in the part to begin with. The word 'maid' was getting on my nerves as I'd already been asked to play lots of them, can't imagine why, but my old friend Metin Hüseyin was directing and he had very interesting casting ideas. Instead of the usual suspects from the upper crust of the acting fraternity who dominated lead roles in TV costume dramas, he had a young actor/musician from Manchester, Max Beesley, as Tom Jones and a rising star from working-class Nottingham as leading lady Sophia called Samantha Morton. I was unaware of Max but was already a massive fan of Sam's. I thought she was astonishing so said yes, thank you very much, I'm very happy to play the servant of *that* young lady.

The filming locations were here, there and everywhere around Lincolnshire, Somerset and Dorset and I remember it being a very jolly time. I loved working with Metin, he was good fun and another pair of safe hands. Samantha was just as brilliant a person as she was an actor, and Max was one of the funniest people I had ever met. He was daft as a brush but also completely dedicated to the work, which was the perfect combination.

About halfway through the shoot I was back at my flat, enjoying a couple of days off. It was a Sunday morning and I was still in my pyjamas as I was a little worse for wear from a drinkie session with Joe Wright the night before, which ended with him pushing me home in a discarded supermarket trolley. I had decided to spend the day doing fuck-all when the phone rang. It was David Thewlis, a friend and brilliant actor who a few years before had made his mark in the film *Naked*. He was in Cannes for the film festival and had seen *Nil By Mouth* the night before. 'It's fucking amazing, it makes *Naked* look like the *Magic* fucking *Roundabout*. Gary's done an incredible job.' I was chuffed. I knew the film was being shown there but couldn't go because of my work commitments to *Tom Jones*, so was relieved it was getting a positive reaction.

Half an hour later the phone rang again, 'Hello, Kathy?'

'Oh, hello, Joan,' I said, thinking it was Auntie Joan Galvin from my childhood.

But, 'Joan?! Who the hell is Joan? It's Gary, Gary Oldman!'

Oh.

He said someone on the judging panel had broken the rules and told him I had won best actress, in order for him to get me over for the award ceremony that evening.

Come again? I was shocked, genuinely 100 per cent shocked. I hadn't thought of Val as a leading role; *Nil By Mouth* was about the men, wasn't it? I'd seen the film a few weeks before Cannes and, as far as I was concerned, Ray and Charlie gave the standout performances. Sure, I was good in it but not *that* good. (A little side story; I took Joe Wright with me to the screening. When Gary asked who he was I confidently replied, 'He'll direct you in a film one day that will win you an Oscar.' And he did.)

As Gary chatted on, I suddenly realised I didn't have a passport.

It had run out and as I hadn't been on holiday I'd had no reason to renew it.

'I can't go,' I said, quietly relieved. 'I don't have a passport.'

Gary was flabbergasted. What the fuck? He told me to stay off the line and not to tell a soul, he would call me back. I put the receiver down and the phone rang again immediately. It was Stephen. Gary's manager, Doug, had spoken to him while Gary was speaking to me.

'Fucking hell,' I said.

'Fucking hell,' Stephen said.

'I can't go,' I said again. 'I don't have a passport.'

Stephen said not to worry about that for now, just pack an overnight bag and sort out something to wear. He would get back to me.

Something to wear? At the Cannes film awards? What the fuck was I going to wear?? I was still in my pyjamas, and as far as I was concerned there was no way I was going to get out there so I carried on staring into space and smoking. An eternity later and I still hadn't moved from my spot on the sofa and hadn't called anyone as I was told not to. Stephen rang.

'Okay, it's happening, I don't know how but it *is* happening! Make sure you're ready as I'll be picking you up in an hour.'

Oh shit. I ran up to the bathroom, showered and bunged the small amount of make-up I had into a bag along with clean knick-knocks and a nightie. I threw open my wardrobe door and there, fresh from the dry cleaner's, was a pinstriped bespoke suit I'd had made for Harry Enfield's wedding a few weeks earlier. Phew. I found a crisp white shirt and thought, *It's not a frock but fuck it, that'll do*. I was ready and waiting with half an hour to spare so I called John and then Elaine. They were both giddy. I stipulated they couldn't say a word to *anybody* but told John to tell Barry and for Elaine to absolutely tell Tilly.

Stephen arrived and we were driven to City Airport, where a small private jet provided by Luc Besson (who was one of the film's producers) was waiting for us, my lack of passport not being a problem in those pre-9/11 days. Stephen was tickled pink that the pilot carried our bags.

As we flew over the English Channel it finally hit me and I thought I was going to throw up. We arrived at Nice Airport, where a young French lady greeted us on the tarmac. 'Bonjour, bonjour! Time is running out so you will go to the helicopter!'

I stopped in my tracks, no, no, no, I did *not* want to go in a helicopter, thank you!

'The traffic is BIG so you *must* go to helicopter!'

And before we knew it, Stephen and I were flying over the French Riviera in a glass-bottomed helicopter on a journey that lasted no more than ten minutes. We were then in another car where we joined a cavalcade, with the streets on either side lined with cheering people.

Flipping heck.

We pulled up outside Palais des Festivals and its famous red-carpeted stairs. Luc Besson opened my car door, kissed both cheeks, then Gary was by my side, holding my hand and saying into my ear above the cheering throng, 'It's a bit different to our digs in Westcliff, love.'

The rest of the night is a blur of receiving the award from Hugh Grant, giving a press conference along with Sean Penn, who had won best actor, having a million photos taken by millions of photographers, asking Kylie Minogue if she'd like to join our table for dinner as she and her then-boyfriend couldn't find their own, accepting a Bellini cocktail from Harvey fuckface Weinstein and going for a way-past-midnight stroll in the grounds of Hotel du Cap with David Thewlis, who couldn't believe his eyes when he saw me on the red carpet after talking with me on the phone just a few hours earlier. I think that's what they call a whirlwind.

It was now close to three in the morning and we were back at Gary's villa, where I was more than relieved to see a packet of PG Tips teabags sitting beside a kettle. I went to bed, didn't sleep and honestly thought, *What the fuck is going to happen now?*

THE DAYS AFTER

A few hours later, Stephen and I were travelling first class on a British Airways flight where upon boarding I received a round of applause from the crew and passengers, and Stephen made everyone laugh by pretending the applause was for him.

A car was waiting for us and in it were most of the day's newspapers, with my grinning face on the front pages and articles filled with quotes of stuff I couldn't remember saying.

We were driving up the back of King's Cross when I realised the direction the driver was taking. It was 10 a.m., the time Anna Scher opened the office, so I asked if we could do a little stop-by. Looking back, that's the thing I'm most proud of. Anna was delighted with me, 'Kathy, darling! We are all so thrilled! How wonderful!' She gave Stephen a big hug too, which made him very happy.

Stephen dropped me back at the flat and said he'd call later. I called out for George, who came bounding down the road after being out all night, which wasn't unusual. I fed him, made myself a cuppa and sat back in the same spot I'd been in just twenty-four hours earlier.

The answer machine blinked with over fifty messages. I switched it on. Some were clear and full of excitement and congratulations, but as it went on the messages were getting scrambled and the last twenty or so cut out before they began. I unplugged it, took the phone off the hook and lay with George on the sofa, hoping for a bit of sleep, when the *knock-knock-knocks* came and with them a constant stream of flowers, champagne and telegrams.

A bit later Tilly and Elaine came over and we had fish and chips. The girls said we needed a proper celebration so said they would do a ring round and tell everyone we'd be in the Old Red the following Sunday.

Newspapers and TV shows wanted interviews. I decided to speak to the *Islington Gazette* and to chat with lovely Richard and Judy on *This Morning*.

Then it was back to work on *Tom Jones*. I can't remember where we were but when I arrived at the hotel room it was filled to the brim with flowers. Samantha Morton had apparently done a whip-round. This was of course extremely thoughtful but I soon realised I couldn't breathe because the flowers were sucking the oxygen out of the room, so they had to be got rid of.

I went for a walk with friend and fellow cast member Matt Bardock. I think Matt was the first person I told all the above from start to finish. His beautiful, huge, blue eyes nearly popped out of his face as he listened, and we laughed our heads off.

The Sunday at the Old Red was a riot. Anyone who could make it, did. John, Barry and Carm were there, and Simon and Rowly from Raw Sex, plus most of the old regular gang. Somebody asked me to give a speech so I stood on a table, thanked everyone for coming and shouted happily, 'The drinks are on the house!' Landlord Tony went white, and I realised I should've said, *The drinks are on* me.

A week or so later and things still hadn't calmed down. Any time off from *Tom Jones* was spent either giving interviews to help promote *Nil By Mouth*, reading through a pile of scripts with offers of work or going for meetings with film directors about potential work. The press interviews were the worst. I was suddenly *Nil By Mouth*'s spokesperson and one time got hoodwinked into saying something silly and personal when the interview had supposedly 'finished'. Lesson learned.

In the space of a month my life had changed dramatically, but I wasn't as happy as I should've been.

A RELUCTANT FILM STAR

Before you start shouting 'You ungrateful bitch!' I want to stress I *was* extremely grateful for what had happened but I wasn't prepared, as I certainly hadn't expected it.

Stephen said I could now do whatever I wanted, and what I wanted was more theatre work, but it was only film offers that headed my way and decisions had to be made quickly. We went to Dublin to meet director Pat O'Connor for a film version of Brian Friel's play *Dancing at Lughnasa*, and then back to London for a meeting with Shekhar Kapur who would be directing *Elizabeth* with rising star Cate Blanchett in the lead and wanted me to play Queen Mary, a small but significant role. I had very interesting meetings with both, particularly Shekhar. I already knew quite a bit about Bloody Mary from my Catholic upbringing and felt her 'madness' was more likely due to her being in excruciating pain from cancer than anything else, and he agreed. It felt like a meeting of minds and I couldn't wait to work with him, but first I set off for the Emerald Isle.

I had very romantic notions about Ireland. I always felt that when I eventually got there I wouldn't want to return to London and would end up making it my home, but that wasn't the case.

We were a lovely cast, including the brilliant Bríd Brennan (who had already won a Tony Award for her performance in the stage version), Sophie Thompson, Catherine McCormack, Rhys Ifans, Michael Gambon and big fat movie star Meryl Streep. Director, Pat, was a good guy, but something didn't feel right to me and now, nearly thirty years on, I can't fully explain why but I fucking hated it. There was a snooty atmosphere caused by its very bumptious producer Noel Pearson, who kept patronising me by parading me around to anyone who'd listen, saying my Donegal accent was remarkable, 'Listen to the way she speaks in real life!' This wasn't flattering as I was an actor so what the fuck did he expect? I felt he thought I was just some working-class oik who'd been plucked from obscurity by Gary Oldman and, as much as I liked Pat O'Connor, I realised sometime later, he must've felt the same way when he admitted he'd only seen *Nil By Mouth* and none of my other work. Basically, I got the job because I was of Irish heritage and I'd won at Cannes, and that felt a bit shit after nearly two decades' worth of graft.

As a cast we got on well, but I felt like a puppet rather than an actor. Any ideas or contributions were dismissed and the set felt more like a church than the family home it should've been. Our characters were sisters but the constant shouting of 'Quiet on set!', even when it was already very fucking quiet, quashed any chance of finding a natural camaraderie. I remember Pat questioning my unhappiness and asking what he could do to lift my spirits and I said, 'Could you give me the sack, please?' He couldn't.

Tilly and Elaine came over for a weekend, which was great, and so did John and his then girlfriend Beth. These visits were much needed and appreciated as I felt I was, once again, losing my mind.

We were staying in The Westbury hotel, which had a large lounge area with a grand piano and a smaller bar-room to the side. It was posh and very nice but living in a hotel for weeks on end isn't as lovely as staying in one for a couple of nights.

One weekend, Max Beesley came over. We'd become great pals on *Tom Jones* and I missed his daftness. He loved Gambon and was itching to make his acquaintance. I introduced them in the bar and Michael politely said hello then turned his attention elsewhere. Max was lusting after the beautiful piano in the lounge, desperate to have a go, but when I asked, the concierge rather haughtily replied, 'Oh no, we couldn't possibly allow that.' Maybe he thought I wanted Max to bash out 'My Old Man's a Dustman' or something similar? When the hired pianist finished his vanilla plinking, though, I elbowed Max and told him to ignore the rules and just get on it. So he did.

What followed was like a scene from a movie. Max sat down, stretched his fingers and started to play, rather beautifully, Bach's Prelude in C minor. No disrespect to the hired bloke beforehand but I could tell this was of a different class, and so could everyone else. The people in the lounge stopped talking and turned to look, and the people in the bar stood up and started to wander over and gather around the piano, including Gambon. The piece ended with a huge round of applause.

Gambon asked Max, 'Can you play me some Erroll Garner?'

Max replied, 'Of course I can, Garner is the boss.'

Then proceeded to elegantly play 'Misty', with Michael now sitting beside him on the stool, looking at Max and his masterful playing with a delighted smile and dewy eyes. Another round of applause and I felt so proud of my brilliant friend.

We were now a couple of weeks away from the end of the shoot. I was awake very early one Sunday morning and went for a walk. When I returned, the concierge, who was now my pal after Max's impromptu concert, asked if I'd heard about the princess? I thought he was telling me a joke and was waiting for the punchline but . . . Back in my room I turned on the TV to the news that Princess Diana had been killed in a car crash. I rang Rhys then Catherine and they came to my room. I knocked on Michael's door, he opened it, dishevelled from his sleep, and gave his usual joke of, 'Have you put in for your right to buy yet?' I asked if he'd heard the news, which he hadn't, and he said, 'Bloody hell.' He joined us in my room and the four of us stayed mostly silent as we watched the news for the next couple of hours. I wasn't a royalist, but the sadness I felt for Diana's children ran deep. It made me think of my own brothers losing their mum at such a young age. Catherine had also lost her mother as a child and we looked at each other with a sad recognition. When they left, I called John.

I was glad when the job was over and I was now sitting in a make-up chair with genius designer Jenny Shircore at Shepperton Studios. *Elizabeth* had already been filming for a couple of months and my role was only going to take a few days to shoot. I was taken to set and was looking forward to seeing Shekhar Kapur, but it was like meeting a completely different person. He was talking to me as if I were an imbecile. Slow and measured instructions, along with line reading me as if I were a child. I was befuddled. When we broke for lunch I asked if there was a chance we could have a private chat, so Shekhar came to my dressing room, where I politely asked why he was talking to me as if I were an idiot. His answer shocked me.

'I didn't know when we met that you are working class. People have been telling me that you are not the type of actor who would usually play a queen, so I thought maybe you would need some extra help.'

I should've just laughed, as in hindsight it's so fucking ridic-ulous. But instead I thought, *Is this how it's always going to be for me? Paraded around like a fascinating little monkey or patronised like I'm a fucking halfwit?* I assured him that I didn't need any 'extra help' and was perfectly capable of understanding the workings of the human being I was portraying, despite her status.

Shekhar then got a little upset and said he didn't mean to offend me and he seemed to be upsetting a lot of people and his intentions were only for the good. 'Oh right,' I said, 'I'm glad it isn't just me you're pissing off.'

Later that day there was a knock on my door and Gary Oldman popped his head round. He was working on something in one of the other studios.

'Hello, love, how you getting on?'

'It seems to be okay now,' I said, 'but it got a bit tricky with Shekhar earlier.'

To which Gary replied, 'Oh dear, it never rains but it Kapurs!'

RSVP

The requests for my company were extraordinary. Among them, Formula One, Royal Ascot and the polo, all very Jilly Cooper. Elton John was having a party (when wasn't he?) and Downing Street invited me to a celebration of Labour's recent general election victory. I didn't go to any of them.

I loved Elton John as much as the next person and, to some extent, the Labour Party, but finding time with pals was difficult enough so spending any spare time with people I didn't know wasn't on the agenda. Plus, I liked to party the proper way by getting mightily pissed, having shouted and sometimes heated conversations and laughing and dancing till dawn. This behaviour wasn't really appreciated at high-end dos, as I found out when myself, Tilly and Elaine went to a party at Noel Pearson's home while in Dublin. It was a very precious evening with well-to-do folk giving poetry recitals and the like. Us girls were asked to do something so we sang the song from an advert for Toblerone chocolate. It didn't get the laughs we thought it would and after a couple of heated debates we were eventually asked to leave.

The local cabbie who took us back to the hotel told us, 'The people who frequent that house are the biggest snobs in the whole of Ireland so you're better off out of it!'

It was the era of Britpop and Cool Britannia and I graced the cover of lads' mag *Loaded* after they awarded me with a Woman of the Year trophy.

There was another big party at some point for either *Loaded* or something similar and I went along with a friend, Paulie. It was a daytime event and I didn't usually drink during the day but decided a couple would help ease any anxiety that came along with these things. I was having quite a good time, chatting with interesting folk, when the gorgeous and super talented Rowetta from the Happy Mondays came over and said Shaun Ryder wanted to meet me. How lovely. I sat with him for a bit while he rambled at me incoherently and took from him an inviting-looking spliff which he didn't offer. I took a couple of large drags, thought, *This northern grass tastes off*, said it was nice to meet him then went back to find Paulie. He was stood talking with a gossip columnist from one of the tabloids. I remember feeling really fucking weird and did something horrible that Paulie relayed to me the following day. I sat down next to where they were chatting and held my cigarette underneath the young lady's bottom. When she eventually felt the heat from it she jumped up and quite rightly shouted at me, 'What the fuck are you doing?!'

Paulie also had a go, 'Kath! That's fucking out of order!'

I then called them a couple of cunts and headed for the door, where I pushed a paparazzi bloke over and got into a cab. When I got home I was violently sick and had hot and cold shakes. The last time I'd felt that way was when I was around sixteen and had a drink spiked at a gig. I got myself home safely that time too.

My wayward behaviour was obviously written about in the newspaper and hopefully I apologised but I can't remember if I did.

Cut to many years later and I was in Shaun Ryder's company again while we were doing a TV show. I asked him what might've been in that spliff as I had a feeling it couldn't have just been weed. He confirmed this with the very casual reply of, 'Back then? Nah, it wouldn't have been weed, it was either smack or quite possibly crack.'

No excuse, but it made me feel a wee bit better there was a genuine reason I had turned into a spun-out, mad twat.

AND THE WINNER ISN'T . . .

The premier of *Nil By Mouth* took place while I was in Ireland so I couldn't go. Stephen and the *Lughnasa* production team tried their best but sometimes that's just the way things are.

Moya phoned and filled me in on all the gossip and said it was a great night. The reviews were mostly favourable but a little patronising here and there, what a surprise. Some thought it must've been improvised as the performances were so natural and is it actually acting when we're so similar to our characters? I personally only improvised two tiny moments and as far as I could tell most of the dialogue was from the original script. Plus, you never saw posh actors critiqued in that way, so why were we?

After *Mr Thomas* was televised I had a meeting with a TV director who wanted to work with Ray but was worried that he might be 'unmanageable' and how 'frightening' was he to work with? I just laughed and said, 'He's an *actor* and obviously a brilliant one if you're so convinced by his performance.' This class divide in the industry was really fucking annoying.

A few months before all the Cannes hoo-ha I read an interview with actress Helena Bonham Carter. In it she complained that she was typecast and wasn't taken seriously and that it was much *easier* for 'non-pretty, working-class actors'. Now, I knew all about being taken out of context, so I checked with a couple of friends of hers if she *really* felt that way. She did and I thought it was pretty outrageous on a couple of counts: firstly, she had been working consistently since the age of sixteen and secondly, she had no clue what it was like to actually struggle in the industry. I had to write a fucking play to prove I had a brain in my head so why didn't she do the same? We were *all* typecast, but to say it was easier for my tribe was a tad unthinking. I composed a letter to *Time Out* magazine that said, 'As a lifelong member of the non-pretty working classes I'd like to say to Helena Bonham Carter, shut up you stupid cunt.' Catherine Wearing popped by the flat for a cuppa and I showed her what I had written. She laughed until she cried, said I absolutely had to send it in, so we went to the postbox together.

The fuss afterwards was interesting. Stephen was impressed but also worried it could jeopardise future work, but I wasn't bothered about that as I wouldn't want to work with anyone who was in agreement with Helena anyway. A journalist friend, Tim Burke (no relation), rang and said I must be prepared for it being brought up in interviews for evermore. He was right.

Cut to some months later and what I hadn't foreseen was that Helena and I would be nominated for a BAFTA in the same category, Best Actress, and in the same year. It was cool, though, because Judi Dench was also nominated, so I knew she was absolutely going to be the winner. And she was. The only reason I was sad not to win was Hugh Grant was presenting and I really wanted to say, 'He gave me one in France.' *Nil by Mouth* won Best British Film and Best Original Screenplay so we had a lovely celebration at the aftershow party. While there, Samantha Morton came over with a naughty twinkle in her eye, 'My friend really wants to meet you.' Then stood aside and revealed Ms Helena Bonham Carter. Oh shit.

I have to say, she was extremely gracious and we had a good chat about it all. I said if she wasn't happy with the roles she was given she could always employ someone to write her something as I was sure she had the means to do so. She hadn't thought of that. She said she actually quite enjoyed one newspaper comparing us to the old-school Hollywood rivalry between the great Joan Crawford and Bette Davis, so I said, 'Well, as long as it's clear I'm Bette we'll be grand.'

WORKING FROM HOME

David Kane was a friend from the Scottish contingent at the Old Red. Back in the late '80s he'd written a wonderful TV film called *Shadow on the Earth*, along with a couple of very funny and surreal plays. Nowadays he's probably best known for writing some of the TV series *Shetland*. Stephen said he was going to direct his latest film, *This Year's Love*, and wanted me for the role of Marey. We had a lovely phone chat while I was in Ireland after I'd read his script, which I loved. He was a bit stuck on the casting for one character, so I suggested Catherine McCormack could be great and was also a top woman and a pleasure to work with. I passed my script on to her and luckily for Davie she loved it too.

The rest of its ensemble were a great bunch; Jennifer Ehle, Ian Hart, Douglas Henshall and Dougray Scott. We were shooting in London so it was especially nice to be home every evening as I was sick and tired of hotel living.

My character was a singer in a band and I spent a couple of very interesting days with singer-songwriter David Gray, who provided music for the film along with it being named after one of his songs. He was extremely patient with me as I wasn't very comfortable with singing. The only other time I'd had to sing was opening the Mike Leigh play I was in with an old music-hall number called 'It's a Great Big Shame', but this time was more nerve-wracking as I had to sing in front of the bloke who actually wrote the stuff. He didn't break down and cry when he heard my rough old tones but said, rather diplomatically, 'You're making this your own.' Very Louis Walsh.

The shoot was a happy one. We loved and respected Davie, and he us. As the film was about trying to find love, we all had a few smoochy scenes. One involved myself and Dougray's character having a snog on Waterloo Bridge, and still to this day that beautiful man will say in interviews that his most enjoyable screen kiss was with me. Likewise, baby! What a dreamboat.

I did a small role in another big ensemble piece, cabbies' favourite *Love Honour and Obey*, and a few TV interviews as myself. The best one of these was Graham Norton's very first episode of his chat show, which was originally on Channel 4. The other guests were Ivana Trump and Sooty and Sweep. During my interview Graham took from his pocket a cutting from a magazine called 'Take a Shit' or some such. Before selfies and social media, publications asked their readers to send in photos of themselves with a celebrity and if printed would be rewarded with a prize. While we were in Dublin, Elaine, who was always up for the craic, said, 'Come on, Kath, let's have a photo done and I'll send it in and see if they print it.' They did, along with a few words from Elaine praising how lovely I'd been when she approached me and how down to earth I was.

Graham, who knew this full well, held the piece up to camera, 'You were very nice to this woman in Ireland. Who is she, by the way?'

'That's my best friend, Elaine,' I said. 'She won twenty pounds and a bottle of champagne, which I really enjoyed drinking with her.'

SICKNESS AND WEALTH

I loved my little flat but was now earning enough money to buy my own place. I could've bought the flat from Islington Council but this didn't feel right to me so I gave it back.

I was on the lookout on and off for about a year until I finally settled on the house I'm still living in now. When I was a kid I loved going to Highbury Fields and imagined living in one of the houses that overlooked them, but these were above my price range and a bit too grand, so I opted for a more modest Victorian terrace just a stone's throw away. My money husbands, Howard and Philip, encouraged me to put down a large enough deposit to give me a mortgage that wouldn't make me wince at the monthly payments.

A beautiful and good-spirited former actor called Guy Scantlebury was now doing house renovations and he, along with a team of very jolly men, put in new floorboards and mantelpieces sourced from salvage yards and lovingly decorated in the colours of my choice.

I moved in early 1999 and spent the first few days kissing the walls. I couldn't believe how my life had changed. I was doing a job I (sometimes) loved and now semi-owned my own home. I think Dad would've been very proud.

Marianne and Evan had their own new home too, along with a bundle of joy called Pascale, so I'd make the journey across London to Dulwich for the great cooking and the added bonus of squishy cuddles, and I of course spent as much time with Billy as I could. I loved taking him to the pictures or the park but didn't enjoy so much sitting in shitty McDonald's, where he'd happily chomp on smelly chicken nuggets while I tried not to barf.

America was calling. Stephen said a few offers had come in and going to Hollywood seemed like the natural next step to take, but I had important stuff going on at home and was reluctant to leave, so I didn't.

John was now working as a graphic designer when his kidney problem reared its head again, so he was put on dialysis. When he visited me in Dublin he sent boxes of the stuff ahead, which lived in my room until he and Beth arrived. Michael Gambon stood in my room in wonder, looking at the pile of boxes containing the peritoneal dialysis that would help keep John alive. 'Fucking hell,' he said, 'isn't science an incredibly beautiful thing.'

John would eventually need a transplant, so I of course volunteered to be tested to see if I was a potential match. I wasn't. There was something awry with my own blood, which was a mystery to the docs back then and it would be a few more years before I found out what that was. In the meantime, John waited patiently for a donor until one finally came, but it was a dud, which was agonising emotionally and physically. As John himself said, 'It's like someone put a lump of old meat into my system so the rest of my body was screaming for it to fuck off!'

Then a year or so later a non-cancerous growth was discovered on his adrenal gland, so this too had to be removed. He spent a couple of weeks recovering at mine, so it was very handy that I now had a spare room. I never cooked meat but made an exception for John. I'd flash-fry minute steaks and, along with a jacket potato and some greens, this would be his requested staple because, 'It's absolutely fucking delicious, Kath!' It felt good to pay him back a wee bit for all the care and cooked meals he'd provided when we were kids. He eventually received a perfectly healthy and matching kidney and we all breathed a huge sigh of relief.

The millennium was looming so I decided to have a party that would double as a house-warming. As most venues were charging big entry fees, Tony and Pauline from the Old Red decided to do the same, the only problem being most of the regulars were coming to mine for free so they weren't selling any tickets. I gave Pauline a ring and said why didn't they come to mine as well and take the night off? She said but what about her daughter Joanne and her husband Paul and Paul's nan? They could come too, I said. So they did, and we all had a great night.

My fondest memory from it was Tilly, Ade and Billy, along with their latest family addition, the magnificent Georgie, staying over. I let them have my room as it had the biggest bed. When I took a peek in the morning, they were all still sound asleep, with Ade hanging off one side, Tilly off the other and the two kids bang in the middle with limbs akimbo as if they were making snow angels in their dreams.

JAM SANDWICH

After I won at Cannes, Harry Enfield called. He was delighted with my win and said because of it he'd be able to get the funds for a Kevin and Perry movie, if I'd be up for it? Too right, mate! *Harry Enfield and Chums* had come to a natural end when Paul decided to produce his own brilliant creation, *The Fast Show*, with Charlie Higson and Caroline Aherne among the cast, so doing a film would be the perfect way to say a proper goodbye to my beloved Perry.

I wasn't involved with writing the script as I couldn't find time with my work schedule, but Harry and writer Dave Cummings did a great job. Some of our gang from the series were on board, including our fabulous costume designer Denise Simmons and her equally fabulous assistant Michelle, along with genius hair and make-up designer Annie McEwan and her lovely assistants Andrea and Petrona.

Ed Bye was our kind and patient director and the sometimes grumpy but mostly giggly Alan Almond our fantastic director of photography.

We shot in London, Watford and, of course, Ibiza, which was a completely different place to the one I'd filmed in ten years earlier.

We'd gone through various actors playing Kevin's dad for TV, but the film version gave us the best, in my humble opinion, the rather brilliant James Fleet, and thankfully the sublime Louisa Rix was available to continue her role as Kevin's mum, known lovingly as Mrs Patterson. I had the best on-screen romance with Louisa. Over the course of the series we'd developed a little twinkle between our characters. Perry was very in lust with Mrs Patterson and she very in amusement with him. It was always great fun working with her.

Another magnificent creature, Rhys Ifans, joined us for the film, as the horrible nemesis to our teenage heroes, superstar DJ Eye Ball Paul. I'd first met Rhys a few years before when he was in a play directed by Michael Sheen. Top photographer Rankin was co-founder and editor of trendy magazine *Dazed and Confused* and had asked if I would interview an up-and-coming person of my choice, so I chose Rhys. We had a lovely afternoon and sometime later did *Dancing at Lughnasa* together, which, as we already know, wasn't a good time for me, so it felt really satisfying to be his work colleague again when I felt happy and more like myself. God, we had fun. The crew were also a lively bunch and we'd all congregate together in a bar at the end of a day's filming in Ibiza and drink Rhys's invention, Choccy-Woccy, which was a lethal brandy, vodka and milk chocolate concoction that went down far too easily yet caused no hangover the next morning.

Because we were playing a couple of hormonal, randy teenagers, Harry and I were fitted with electronic penises that worked by remote control. Sexy ladies walked past and *de-boing!*, up went the appendages.

However, the new accessory for most people was a mobile phone, and if someone's went off *de-boing!* it proved very difficult getting through the scene.

I loved every moment of that job. When we were in Watford the total eclipse of the sun happened and we stopped filming to take in this historic event along with a bunch of supporting artists including lots of kids. We oohed, aahed and cheered together as we watched the beautiful darkening from our spot in the not-so-beautiful open-roofed Harlequin shopping centre. No offence, Watford.

Another indication that these were pre-9/11 days was being allowed a visit to the cockpit on the plane to and from Ibiza. It was better on the way home as it was night-time and I marvelled at seeing Heathrow's lit-up runway from as far away as Kent.

When we did the press junket to publicise the film, I was surprised by a couple of journos who suggested that maybe doing this kind of comedy movie was a bit lowbrow compared with the serious stuff I'd been in and why would I make such a choice? This attitude was nonsensical to me. Perry was partly *my* creation and, as I was now a woman in my mid-thirties, when else would I have the opportunity to play a 14-year-old boy?! Besides, a lot of the parts I'd been offered since Cannes were, for the most part, extremely boring, either carbon copies of what I'd done before or roles that I just wasn't right for, with producers seeing me more as a commodity than an actor. Over the years I've definitely turned down more money than I've earned and it's purely because I've done what I wanted to do rather than what people thought I *should* be doing. Catherine Wearing had been encouraging me to turn *Mr Thomas* into a film, as being a film director seemed like the obvious next step to take, but this idea never fully appealed to me. I liked the smallness of theatre. Films could involve hundreds of people plus the added pressure of budgets etc. – and I'd later witness it nearly send Gary Oldman over the edge – so I was happy to dismiss the idea.

ANOTHER BURKE

Barry and Carm had a baby. It was good of them to wait till the year 2000 as it makes it nice and easy to remember his age. Louis was and still is an intelligent and gorgeous human. They were now living in Leytonstone, as Barry thought it was ridiculous how expensive Islington had become, so moved to a lovely house near the Leyton Orient football ground.

Louis was a very happy baby, full of squeaks and giggles, and by the age of one was obsessed with hats, plonking whichever was favourite of the day and of his own choosing on top of his head from the moment he woke to sleepy bedtime. Hence my nickname for him being Louis the Hat, which made him sound like a gangster. This obsession soon wore off, though, so instead the family nickname, given to him by Carm's dad because Lou had a curious and mischievous look in his eyes, was and still is Puck. God, I love that kid, but the most beautiful thing for me was seeing the love between himself and Barry. My brother, who had no proper guidance or tangible expressions of love from our own dad, fell into the role of fatherhood with ease and utter enjoyment. Carm was the feeder, fattening Louis up with porridge and home-steamed veg, but Barry was the squeezer and bedtime story reader and he loved every minute of it.

I'd often thought about having a baby myself. I was in my late thirties so the old clock was ticking, but it wasn't something I was crying out for. I'd been through a short broody spell in my early thirties but wasn't interested in having a child with the person I was with at that time.

Looking back, there was more of an expectation for women

to *want* children, so I think I was feeling a social pressure more than a personal desire. Looking ahead, I found out in my early forties that I wasn't able to have children, my blood condition being a major factor (this accounted for a miscarriage I once had), so I'm actually grateful that having a baby had never been my true heart's calling. Plus, what would I do with constant company? I don't think I could've handled it. I love babies and I've had lovely relationships with the kids in my life, but I'm always happier once I hand them back, and much the same can be said for romantic relationships. The bad love definitely accounted for some trust issues and thwarted a bravery, but going through the motions of being with someone purely because it was something you were *supposed* to do wasn't really my bag. So I didn't. The odd fling was more than enough.

Much like when I was a kid, I was genuinely happy in my own company. Sure, I am and always have been gregarious, I love being with friends or working with a good gang of people, but at the end of the day, shutting the door and sitting with my own thoughts along with a smoke and a cuppa was and still is when I'm at my most content.

PUMP UP THE BASE

Jonathan Harvey had been approached by TV company Tiger Aspect to see if he wanted to write a sitcom. James Dreyfus had been approached by Tiger Aspect to see if he wanted to be in a *new* sitcom after his successful outing as PC Goody in *The Thin Blue Line*. And I asked Stephen to approach Tiger Aspect to let them know I'd had enough of doing films for the moment and instead really wanted to do a sitcom – with hopefully Jonathan as its writer and James as its co-star. It was all very serendipitous.

Jonathan came up with the idea of two misfits sharing a flat: Tom, an actor and an arsehole, and Lindy, just an arsehole. He called it *Gimme Gimme Gimme* because they were both in desperate need of a man and *not* just after midnight.

In the flat upstairs lived Jez and Suez, played by the fabulous Brian Bovell and Beth Goddard, and our formidable ex-sex worker landlady, Beryl Merit, was the much-sought-after and unparalleled Rosalind Knight. Sue Vertue was our producer and Liddy Oldroyd our director.

For the first series I think we were very much trying to find our feet. The premise was Tom and Lindy met on the club circuit while high on MDMA and now, unemployed and with rotten personalities and very little money, were stuck with each other. James and I loved over-the-top clowning and farce so this was the direction we wanted to go in, hence Lindy's bonkers wig and outfits provided by make-up artist Marella Shearer and costume designer Christopher Marlowe. We loved *The Young Ones* and *Bottom* and hated sanitised US sitcoms such as *Friends*, so wanted to be as ugly and as vile to each other as the censor would allow. Jonathan didn't hold back. Liddy was a fantastic and encouraging director but Sue mostly looked worried.

The first couple of episodes didn't go down too well, in fact some people I spoke to hated it, but it had enough fans who appreciated its bawdy and base humour to be commissioned for a further two seasons and a millennium special. Sadly, our wonderful director Liddy became very sick during our second series and had to step aside for our third. We missed her enthusiastic and jovial spirit.

I loved playing Lindy alongside James's Tom. They were such ridiculous, deluded characters with a mix of sweet ignorance and acid awareness. We really enjoyed breaking the fourth wall and so did our audience, and as its script editor I wanted as much of this as possible, but it frightened the powers that be so we were only allowed to indulge in this so much. It's funny that a few years later one of the BBC's biggest comedy hits, *Mrs Brown's Boys*, was encouraged to fully embrace this concept.

We had some great guests throughout, including friends Moya Brady, Charlie Condou, Ronan Vibert and Elaine Lordan as Lindy's sister, who Jonathan bestowed with the filthy name Sugar Walls. Mark Benton and Chris Simon were in one of my favourite episodes, 'Stiff', which was a little homage to Joe Orton, and Jonathan himself made a couple of appearances, which were silly and hilarious. I wanted him to be in it more, but he was much happier behind the scenes. Very wise.

It became a bit of a cult sensation and some audience members would turn up dressed as the characters for the live recordings, plus we had a local vicar who seemed to be constantly there. Maybe he was secretly asking for his God's forgiveness on our behalf?

Our brilliant and lovely stage manager, Mary Motture, tried to keep things running as smoothly as possible but this often proved difficult if we got the giggles. The worst time for me was when Lindy had the line, 'When I was eight I found Mummy's *Joy of Sex* and I must admit I had a little flick.' For some reason I couldn't stop imagining my childhood hero Irene Handl saying the line and it took a very long time for me to get my act together, leading to studious Mary giving me the sternest of looks and whispering in my ear, 'The audience are getting fed up and quite frankly so am I!' She was the *last* person I wanted to piss off, so I had to dismiss all thoughts of Irene and imagined myself never working again instead.

The show was nominated for quite a few gongs and I won a British Comedy Award. These ceremonies were always a bit rowdy and rebellious so upon receiving my award from the brilliant star of the Airplane films, Leslie Nielsen, I rather arrogantly said, 'It's about fucking time!' which I'm proud to report got the biggest laugh of the night.

There were a lot of people in the comedy industry who looked down on *Gimme*, finding its humour too base and lowbrow and surely we've moved on from that sort of stuff? But Jonathan, James and I cared more about its fan base than them. It was ludicrous and daft and we absolutely loved it, but after one of my breaking-the-fourth-wall moments was cut, despite getting a huge roar and round of applause from the studio audience, James and I decided to call it a day.

Jonathan said later my decision didn't surprise him. He knew I was frustrated with not being listened to. It didn't matter that I was its script editor and gave a few ideas for episode storylines – as far as everyone else was concerned, I was one of its stars and that was that.

It's very different today, where you'll often see actors also be credited as executive producer, meaning their contributions are taken on board and listened to. But, despite my moaning woes, I still look back on that time with a great feeling of fondness.

THREE MORE FILMS

I was back working with Metin Hüseyin, doing a small part in Meera Syal's film adaptation of her own wonderful novel *Anita & Me* and really enjoyed playing horrible Deirdre and being in Metin's company again.

Then it was off to the Isle of Man for *The Martins*, which was written and directed by Tony Grounds. I had a great time on this job. Tony is a lovely writer with the biggest potty mouth I'd ever come across, he makes me sound like an angel. The beautiful Lee Evans played our leading man Robert, I was his long-suffering but loving wife Angie, and the incredible, amazing, best actress in the whole wide fucking world, Linda Bassett, played my mum, Anthea. It was a lovely film but I felt it would've fared better if it had been made for TV rather than cinema.

One evening while having some dinner with Tony and Lee, Tony asked what was the best compliment anyone had given us. It felt a bit wrong to be so showy-offy but Tony insisted, saying, 'Come on, just between us, let's be fucking flash.' I don't think I'd told many people about the time Peter Cook said I was a genius, so I happily relayed the story, thinking they'd be mightily impressed. They were, but Lee said Peter Cook also told him *he* was a genius, then Tony, who had written something Peter Cook was in, said, 'And me, he said *I* was a fucking genius too!' It diluted my story somewhat, knowing Peter Cook seemed to tell most people he came across that they were a bloody genius, but at least he made us feel great about ourselves.

I then headed to Nottingham to work with the very talented director Shane Meadows on *Once Upon a Time in the Midlands*.

The only problem being, so did most of the other 'well-known' actors of the time, including Robert Carlyle, Shirley Henderson and my old pal, Rhys Ifans. No disrespect to them or myself, but this wasn't the way Shane usually worked. He was known for *discovering* stars such as the brilliant Paddy Considine, Stephen Graham and Vicky McClure, but I think he was pressured by producers, which was a big mistake as the film is his only flop. We fucking ruined it. Star power? Star shower more like.

The world changed the day Rhys and I took the train together to start the job, on 11th September 2001, and we found ourselves once again in a hotel room, watching the news unfold.

My world was changing too. I was becoming increasingly unhappy with just being an actor and really wanted to focus on more theatre directing. I'd done a job between these films that confirmed this for me, which was one of the happiest and most fulfilling since *Nil By Mouth*.

OVER AND OUT?

Jenny Topper, the illustrious artistic director of the Hampstead Theatre, where I'd done *Amongst Barbarians* and *The Boys Next Door*, had commissioned Jonathan to write a new play for them in conjunction with Birmingham Repertory Theatre and she asked if I'd like to direct. I would've said yes without reading it but thought I should show an air of professionalism so read it, loved it and said absolutely yes please and thank you.

Out In the Open was set in the garden flat belonging to protagonist Tony during a long weekend. A gay man whose lover had died some time before, Tony was now in search of love again and the play opens with a post-pub drink in the garden with potential new lover, Iggy. Tony has a flatmate, drug-loving Kevin, a friend, self-indulgent Monica, and constant unwanted visits from his dead partner's mother, Mary, and her elderly pal, Rose.

It was very funny of course but also tender and poignant.

There was more freedom with casting back then, meaning Jonathan and I could cast who we felt were best for the roles rather than having the added pressure of nowadays that demands a production to be led by already established 'stars' from film and television. I knew as soon as I finished reading that Linda Bassett had to be Mary. She was up there as one of my favourite actors, as I'd seen seen her be quite magnificent in a few plays at the Royal Court in London, including the original production of Ayub Khan Din's brilliant *East Is East*, and I loved working with her on *The Martins*, so Jonathan and I were more than thrilled when she agreed to do the role. Mark Bonnar was new to me and everyone, but after encouragement from my agent,

Stephen, who represented him (more good taste), we met him, loved him and offered him the role of Tony. We were already fans of Michele Austin and Vilma Hollingbery so they were our Monica and Rose, and after a recommendation from Liza Tarbuck who had just been working with him, Sean Gallagher was our drug-fan flatmate, Kevin.

The part of Iggy was more difficult to find. He was a young Mancunian who had to go through a myriad of emotions, and we saw some lovely actors but none of them possessed the certain 'it factor' we were hoping for. The end of our casting time was looming and we were getting a little anxious when we heard about a young unknown called James McAvoy who was keen to audition. In he came, a bit late and flustered, full of apologies but with an incredible energy and a very thick Scottish accent. This worried me somewhat as Mark's character, Tony, was Scottish, so I asked James if he was able to do a Manchester accent. He looked at me like he wanted to smash my face in and said, again in his very thick Scottish brogue, 'Aye, not a problem!'

He read a couple of scenes with Jonathan and there he was, Iggy, just as we hoped for but more. He was absolutely fucking brilliant and, without needing to even look at Jonathan, never mind have a discussion, I said, 'I think we would love to offer you the part.'

And Jonathan said, 'I'm in total agreement with Kath.'

After a couple of nerve-wracking days waiting, James accepted the role. When Tilly's Manchester-born husband Ade came to see the play with Till, he said afterwards, mightily impressed, 'That kid isn't doing a Manchester accent, he's doing a bloody Cheadle Hulme accent!' But enough of my exuberance as I'm in danger of sounding like one of those patronising arseholes from my past.

It was a very happy rehearsal period. The cast got on so well and were beautifully supportive of each other. There's a big physical fight between the three boys in the play's penultimate scene, and I called in Ray Winstone to act as fight director, which the boys loved.

Our brilliant veteran cast member, Vilma, gave me an invaluable lesson in taking my time in breaking the scenes down. I'd get so carried away with enjoyment at watching them work I'd forget to stop the action so they could go back over what they'd done and then lock it in, leading to Vilma crying out in despair, 'For goodness' sake, Miss Director, give us a fucking chance!'

We opened to some good reviews and some not so favourable, but it didn't matter (as per) because word of mouth led to a sell-out run, and the same when we took it to Birmingham. It was such a hit at Hampstead that Jenny asked us to go back for another four-week run that also sold out.

I opened the play and topped-and-tailed scenes with music from the first album from new band Doves, called *Lost Souls*. So many people asked about the music as they were leaving the theatre that we eventually put a cover of the CD with info about the band on display in the bar.

All the cast were excellent, but Linda Bassett was phenomenal, giving a truth and earthiness to her performances like no other. She really can't be matched. Our stage management and bar staff girls were great fun and would join the cast most nights after the show for a drink in a restaurant up the road called The Globe. This was run by two accommodating gay guys who would lock the doors once paying customers had left and let everyone drink till the early hours. The girls liked to do dance routines to the latest pop songs, and lovely Kylie Minogue, who had seen the play twice, went off with them for a bit then came back having taught the girls the routine to 'Spinning Around', and they along with Kylie herself gave us a fantastic performance.

I loved all of the cast, of course, but I became closest with Sean Gallagher. Born and bred in Luton with his Glaswegian mum, Margaret, Dubliner dad, Dessie, and three brothers, he is gay but has a doted-on and marvellous daughter Rhona who came about from a time of love and confusion with his best friend, the wonderful Caroline, when they were in their late teens.

Sean was a brilliant actor but also smart, rebellious and very, very funny. We were smitten and confused with each other for a time but, after a lot of hard work and a few tears, we managed to sort ourselves out, and he and I, along with his eventual beautiful husband Peter, have remained the greatest of friends. I couldn't imagine the past twenty-five years of my life without him.

When the job ended I went back to acting in the aforementioned three films, which I enjoyed – but not fully. I used to love acting so much, but the feeling I'd get in my tummy and the roots from my boots when playing certain roles was dissipating, and everything seemed to be coming from my head instead. I'd been offered more directing work and was sad I couldn't take these on because of my acting commitments.

Whenever I was asked about the difference between acting and directing, usually by black cab drivers, the best analogy I came up with was acting was like being a footballer and directing was being the coach. Then they understood.

I had to make a decision so asked Stephen to come over to the house for breakfast and a big serious chat.

FAME III

Stephen, who knew me so well, knew what I was going to say so I was more than relieved when he jumped in on my nerves before I started talking. 'You want to stop acting, don't you?' he said.

'Yes,' I said, 'but just for a couple of years. I want the directing jobs to take priority over the acting ones but just for a bit. I think I need to *miss* acting, then hopefully my love for it will eventually come back.'

It didn't.

We talked about the fact he wasn't a director's agent and should I join someone who was? But I didn't want to do that. Anyone who needed to already knew I was looked after by Stephen, and I didn't want to confuse things or start a new professional relationship. Plus, I was still getting lots of voice-over work and, as theatre directing paid a pittance in comparison, it was important to keep these going for as long as possible because any savings I'd accumulated would start to run out pretty quickly.

I had some publicity to do for *The Martins*, which included an appearance on the very popular Saturday morning show *SMTV Live*, hosted by the very popular duo Ant and Dec. The queen of pop Madonna had started a fashion trend by wearing a tee shirt with the name 'BRITNEY' blazoned across it in honour of pop sensation Britney Spears. Then the queen of cooking Nigella Lawson followed suit by wearing a tee shirt with the name 'DELIA' across it in honour of beloved British cook Delia Smith. So I had a tee shirt made with the name

'BETTY SWALLOCKS' across it in honour of lowbrow comedy and wore it on the show.

When the boys were summing up the interview and asked what I would be doing next, I announced my intention to stop acting so I could focus on theatre directing, and I saw the light leave their gorgeous Geordie eyes. They couldn't be less interested.

A day or so later I was walking up my street where a young lad, aged around ten, who lived in one of the houses opposite was kicking a football around. I smiled and nodded as per, when he called out to me.

'Excuse me, Kathy, don't you want to be famous any more?'

I stopped, had a think about his question, which amused me, and replied, 'D'you know what? No, I don't think I do.'

He screwed up his little face in disbelief and said, rather pointedly, 'You're mad!'

NEW BEGINNING

I took myself off for some much-needed and long-overdue therapy sessions with a wonderful man called Lee. He loved my mind and assured me that it was very much intact. Stephen said more acting offers had come through and it felt good to say no thank you without reading any of the scripts. A few artistic theatre directors had been in touch and plans were made for meetings, but in the meantime maybe a little break was in order. It had been nearly twenty years since *Scrubbers*. Twenty years filled with scripts and ideas and friends and heartbreak and grief and fun, and I was knackered.

I waited till October, then Sean and I went off on a walking holiday around Cornwall. I loved it being so cold, especially at Land's End, where the biting wind from the Atlantic Ocean stung my cheeks.

I was healthy emotionally, physically and mentally despite my young neighbour's qualms and was looking ahead with genuine excitement. No more working with people I didn't like or respect. I would be making the decisions from now on and any mistakes would lay at my own feet. As I was approaching forty, this seemed like a very grown-up place to be professionally, and on a personal note I was still acting the idiot and having a great time.

The family were doing well and so was my large circle of friends, with more important friendships still to come. I'd had a pretty lucky run of things all in all, and my 'ambition' for the next few years at least was to remain as happy and fulfilled as possible. And I was.

ACKNOWLEDGEMENTS

Special thanks to John and Barry for trusting me with our story. Thanks to early readers Jonathan and Pippa, and to early listeners Elaine and Tom. Thanks also to editors Kat, Clare and Flo, and big, fat thanks to publisher Holly for the unwavering encouragement and lovely lunches. Thanks to all the pals over the years – especially the practically perfect Tilly – and thanks and well done to Billy and Louis for turning into very fine young men.

PICTURE CREDITS

1. Author's parents' wedding day: supplied by the author; author with siblings: courtesy of Barry Burke

2. Author in favourite coat: supplied by the author; author with the Galvins: supplied by the author; author with Pat Cook's parents: supplied by the author

3. Author with Pat Cook: supplied by the author; author with brothers and Pat Cook: supplied by the author; photo booth picture 1: supplied by the author; photo booth picture 2: supplied by the author

4. Author's friend at a gig: supplied by the author; author's brother Barry and his wife: courtesy of Barry Burke; *Scrubbers* still © Moviestore Collection Ltd / Alamy

5. *Sid and Nancy* still © Everett Collection Inc / Alamy; author's twenty-first birthday: supplied by the author

6. Author with Joe Strummer: courtesy of Michèle Winstanley; scan of currency: supplied by author; author in a hotel bar in Nicaragua: supplied by the author; author with Alex Cox 1: supplied by the author; author with Alex Cox 2: supplied by the author

7. Author with three friends in the Old Red pub: courtesy of Michèle Winstanley; author with two friends in the Old Red pub: supplied by the author

8. Author with Perry Fenwick: supplied by the author; author with Rowland Rivron: supplied by the author; author with Simon Brint in the Old Red: courtesy of Michèle Winstanley; Lananeeneenoonoo for Comic Relief: supplied by the author

9. *Amongst Barbarians* programme: scan of The Royal Exchange

Theatre Company printed programme cover; *Home Free!* leaflet: courtesy of Deirdre Strath Clyde; *Mr Thomas* leaflet: supplied by the author; *Mr Thomas* review: scan of cutting from *Time Out* magazine, review by Nicola Robertson; *Mr Thomas* still: supplied by the author

10. Author as Waynetta: supplied by the author; author as Martha in *Mr Wroe's Virgins*: supplied by the author

11. Author's father and Billy: supplied by the author; *Nil By Mouth* still © Album / Alamy; author with Max Beesley: supplied by the author

12. Author with Gary Oldman © Alan Davidson / Shutterstock; author with friends holding award © Malcolm McNally Photography; author in flat: supplied by the author

13. Author with Meryl Streep © Universal Images Group North America LLC / Alamy; *Now* magazine cutting © Future Publishing Ltd; *Elizabeth* still © Moviestore Collection Ltd / Alamy; author in *Loaded* magazine © Getty / Michael Birt / Contributor

14. Author with Mel C © Comic Relief / Contributor via Getty Images; author as Linda La Hughes in *Gimme Gimme Gimme*: supplied by the author; author rehearsing for *Kevin & Perry Go Large*: supplied by the author

15. Billy: supplied by the author; Puck: supplied by the author; Tilly with Georgie and Billy: supplied by the author

16. Mai Zetterling: © United News / Popperfoto / Contributor via Getty Images; Anna Scher © Sheila Burnett